ADDISON COUNTY

JUSTICE

For Robert

Best regards

[signature]

May 1998

ADDISON COUNTY
JUSTICE

TALES FROM A
VERMONT COURTHOUSE

BY

Peter Langrock

INTRODUCTION BY
Patrick Leahy, United States Senator

Paul S. Eriksson, *Publisher*
Forest Dale, Vermont

5   4   3   2   1

Library of Congress Cataloging-in-Publication Data

Langrock, Peter F.
    Addison County justice: tales from a Vermont courthouse /
by Peter F. Langrock.
        p. cm.
    Includes index.
    ISBN 0-8397-0097-0
    1. Trials—Vermont—Addison County. 2. Justice, Administration of—
Vermont—Addison County—History. I. Title.
KF220.L36 1997
347.743'507—dc21   97–20346
                                                                  CIP

Drawings by Trudy J. Seeley and Anna M. Seeley

Contents

Preface

On the 27th day of March, 1996, acting as attorney for Addison County, I turned over to Middlebury College a quitclaim deed to the old courthouse, located at the top of the town square in the village of Middlebury. In 1816, Gamaliel Painter had deeded to Addison County the parcel of land on which the courthouse stood, with the stipulation that the property revert to his heirs if the land should stop being used as a courthouse. In his will he left the residue of his estate to Middlebury College, and thus the college acquired the reversionary interest. When the new courthouse was completed in 1996, the red brick structure that had been built in 1882 ceased to be the county courthouse.

Since starting as a law clerk in 1958, I had gone through the front doors of that courthouse on more than four thousand days to participate in a contested hearing or trial. The community history that had found its way to resolution in the court system during those almost forty years would be lost if not chronicled in some way. Realizing I had a great deal of personal knowledge of what had transpired in that courthouse—the cases and the players—I took on the responsibility of writing its contemporary history.

What I didn't expect was how much fun it would be to think back to the drama, the humor, and the political changes that occurred in the old building during those forty years.

Karl Llewellyn, one of the great law teachers of the twentieth century, taught me when I was a student at the University of Chicago that all case law is in reality the stories of people who had disputes they couldn't resolve, but instead had to look to the courts. In Vermont these disputes often went to the state supreme court or even to the United States Supreme Court for final resolution. The stories of these people and their foibles that made their way to the Addison County Courthouse is the essence of this book.

I know from my practice in other courts in Vermont and other states, as well as from conversations with lawyers across the country, that the stories coming out of this courthouse are not unique to it. Every county courthouse has a similar history, and in every county in this country the courts have played a major role in the history of their community.

I am not a historian by trade or training. I am an attorney and counselor-at-law who helps people deal with the stories of their lives. I have not attempted to write a history of the events themselves as much as to write a history using the stories and the lore of the courthouse.

Lawyers have always had a tradition of fighting fiercely in the courtroom, while maintaining a level of cordiality that often ends up with sharing a drink after the day's work is done. Lawyers love to trade tales while waiting in hallways for a judge, or for a jury to return. At bar meetings these tales get told and sometimes improved for the better telling. These very tales, coming from the lawyers' personal experience, make up the fabric of the history of the community. Nowhere has this tradition been greater than in Addison County. In 1893, Lucius Chittenden, the great-grandson of Vermont's first governor, Thomas Chittenden, and one of the state's leading lawyers of his time, said in an essay in The Green Bag, a magazine for lawyers:

Good fellowship, respect for one another, may make our hardest drudgery pleasant. Once or twice in every year the lawyers of every country

'Should gather round the table
With mirth and uproar loud...'

as we did at the annual bar supper of Addison County, Vermont. There we had in all the judges; we criticized their opinions, made speeches, and sung songs. The memory of those festivals still clings around the old court-house and hotel in Middlebury, and gray-hair sires tell their grandsons of the glorious fun we had at least once a year. Now, forty years afterward, I hear testimony to the fact that nowhere in the State was the hard work of our profession so agreeable, the brethren so courteous to the court and to each other, rivalry and jealousy so completely suppressed among members of the bar in Vermont as in Addison County, These excellent results were largely due to the annual bar supper!

Middlebury is not only a college town but the county seat of the most active agricultural county in the northeast United States, the site of several small manufacturing companies and the home of a healthy tourist industry. Main Street has not changed in any substantial way since I was a boy, and, thankfully, the old courthouse will be preserved in form, if not in function, by Middlebury College.

I started out with my office in the courthouse in 1960 when I was state's attorney of Addison County. The last time I walked through the doors of the courthouse was to witness the production of Dracula by the Middlebury Community Players that was directed by my wife, Joann. The story of Dracula has been told many times. The stories in this book have also been told many times, to a much smaller audience. I believe they are worth sharing, not only with the people from the local community, but with anyone who has an interest in and a passion for the people, and for the changes that occur in a community over a defined period of time.

Introduction
by
Patrick Leahy
United States Senator

Chittenden and Addison counties adjoin each other and it seems the border sometimes does not exist. *Addison County Justice* demonstrates that the cases that pass through a courthouse door, while factually unique, are also representative of tales from every country courthouse in the country.

Peter Langrock spent as much time in the courts in Burlington in Chittenden County defending Addison county accused as he did in Middlebury in Addison County. His stories of defending homicides put in perspective the human side of our work and, also, asides that never make it into the court record. During my tenure as a state's attorney I got to know Peter. I also got to know many more people from Addison county of the "presumed innocent but charged" set than I would have liked.

Peter and I were probably the two youngest state's attorneys our state has had, and we arrived on the scene at a time when not only were we the chief law enforcement officers of our counties, but we were the only prosecutors in the county.

When you are a state's attorney and you do it all, you grow up very fast. For example, I took office one month after my twenty-sixth birthday and immediately was handed a series of murder cases. In one of the earliest, I was called to the scene of a tragedy where it appeared that a homicidal maniac had attacked a family in one of the upscale neighborhoods of Burlington. The mother was seriously injured, with a fractured skull, having been struck with a hammer. The ten-year-old daughter had been stabbed through the heart with a kitchen knife with such power that the tip of the blade came out her back. The father was critically injured by stab wounds, and it was obvious he would not live long. To add to my shock, I recognized the father as someone I had known for some time. I leaned down as the doctors worked on him, and asked, "Who did this?" He looked at me and I was sure he knew the answer to my question, but he just looked away. Knowing the family history, my heart sank, but I persisted in asking the question. "Who did this to you? You know you have to tell me."

He turned back to me and said, "Pat, my son did this." And then he died.

I knew which son he meant and knew he had another son in the Weeks School, a juvenile facility in Vergennes. I immediately had our detectives notify the police in Addison County and sent police officers heading for the Weeks School as fast as they could go. There they apprehended the suspected son as he staggered up the steps to the house where his younger brother was staying, his clothes blood-splattered and he weak from loss of blood from cuts he had received as he stabbed his family. We assumed his younger brother was to be the next victim. . .

One of the joys of Peter's book is the humor that comes out of the everyday practice of law. The stories of the Alice B. Toklas Brownies, the digging up of the scallop truck with the ripe lobster bait, are just the type of thing lawyers love to tell and retell. Among my own cases, my favorite is a story about a man who had been caught in the middle of the night rifling the safe at Cassler's Toy store. The police charged that he went through a basement window and was emptying the money into a pillow case when they arrived. To me it seemed like an open-and-shut case, but a bright young lawyer, fresh out of law school and from a few too many trial tactic post-graduate courses, felt he had a way to win this case. With long and florid motions he subpoenaed the production of the casement from the window his large and burly client was charged with entering. Throughout the case he bored an unimpressed jury with his use of ponderous terminology, all leading up to a theory that his client could not fit through the window casement.

My chief witness was a Sergeant Bouvier who looked like everybody's favorite uncle. Trim, military bearing, gray haired. He took the stand with the air of probity of an archbishop. When asked what he did, he consulted the notes that he meticulously kept the night of the crime, recounting which cruiser he went in, the minute that he logged onto the scene, the view of the broken window, the drawing of his revolver (complete with serial number) and the order to the accused to put up his hands and that he was under arrest. Keeping my back to the jury so that they couldn't see my smile, I asked the sergeant what happened next. He replied that he ordered the accused to come out the same way he went into the building. I then asked him the only question that counted: "And what did he do then, Sergeant?" The sergeant pointed to the window casement prominently marked Respondent's Exhibit A, and said: "He climbed right out through Respondent's Exhibit A."

The judge busied himself behind some papers so the jury couldn't see the smile on his face, the jury did their best to contain themselves; the defending attorney went through a flurry of motions, statements and other obfuscations, the jury was out for a matter of minutes, marched back in, the foreman looked at me and slipped his finger across his throat and, barely containing his glee, he said to the judge, "HE'S GUILTY."

I remember that in the late 1960s and early 1970s the justice system worked very much as Peter describes it in the book. For me it was the most fulfilling part of my life. Predominately honest lawyers, judges and police made things work even though we never had enough resources. What Peter learned from Jack Conley on his first day in court I also learned: that the greatest responsibility of a prosecutor is to know when justice is best served by not bringing a charge as compared to the often easier task of bringing it. Maybe some of the special prosecutors of this generation should have spent some time as lawyers in rural Vermont.

As *Addison County Justice* reminded me of my stories, it will remind every lawyer of the human side of cases they have had, but you don't have to be a Vermont lawyer to enjoy *Addison County Justice*. Peter Langrock writes with clarity, humor and understanding of a fascinating legal career. I thoroughly enjoyed it, and hated to see the book end.

ADDISON COUNTY
JUSTICE

1. Leo Durocher Comes to Town

The public's curiosity about the workings of the courts did not start with the O.J. Simpson case. Before television brought courtroom drama to the home, people often lined up for admission to the courtroom when there was a trial of significant interest, bringing their brown-bag lunches with them. Addison County has not been without its share of these cases.

One of the most famous trials in Addison County took place in 1964. Leo "the Lip" Durocher, a member of the infamous Gas House Gang of the St. Louis Cardinals baseball team, teammate of Dizzy and Paul Dean, coach of the New York Giants when Bobby Thompson hit the home run that was to defeat the Brooklyn Dodgers in 1951, and former significant other of that beautiful sexy actress, Laraine Day, came to Middlebury. The purpose of his visit

3

was to get acquainted with the family and the hometown of Carolyn Morin.

Carolyn was a graduate of Middlebury High School, Class of 1955, a handsome young woman who made a successful career as a model. In fact, she wrote a book entitled *Mannequin*, recording the history of her modeling career. Carolyn had met Durocher on a trip to California when she was trying to expand her career from modeling to the movies. Carolyn's father was René Morin, an accomplished mason. René was born in Normandy, France, and he had a temper reminiscent of the foul weather that marked the day of the Normandy invasion. His wife, Anna, often worked at the Middlebury Inn as a waitress. Besides Carolyn they had three other daughters: Moose, Dynamite, and Paula.

Today René and Anna's relationship would raise questions of uncontrolled domestic violence. René would get angry, strike out, and Anna would be the worse for wear. Somehow they always seemed to reconcile, each time with a bit more reluctance on Anna's part.

When news spread that Leo Durocher was coming to Middlebury, the town was abuzz with excitement. He was coming in over a January weekend for a short stay, and he agreed to talk on Sunday night to the American Legion at their meeting rooms and bar facilities at the south end of Court Street. Everybody in town who had access to the Legion showed up for the talk, and it was a great success. The celebration at the Legion bar continued well after 11:00 p.m., when Leo went to his room at the Middlebury Inn.

At approximately 12:02 a.m. on Monday, a scant hour after Leo had retired, Sheriff Al Chandler, armed with a civil arrest warrant known as *mesne process*, knocked on Leo Durocher's hotel door. Leo had just fallen asleep, but he responded to the knock by asking who was there. When Sheriff Chandler identified himself, Leo opened the door. In 1964 the blue laws of the state of Vermont were still in full force and one could not serve a civil writ on Sunday. Thus, the good Sheriff had waited until 12:02 on Monday to effectuate the service.

The service was something which today seems astonishing. It was a writ to take the body of Leo Durocher and to hold it as security in response to a civil tort claim. At that time, it was standard law that an attorney in good standing with the bar could sign a writ of *mesne process*, upon which a person could be taken into custody to answer to a charge of having willfully committed a harmful act.

Sheriff Chandler said, "Mr. Durocher, I have a warrant, and I'm placing you under arrest. Please come with me." Leo, coming from the uncivilized west of California, had trouble understanding exactly what was happening, but he had no choice but to go along with the sheriff.

Leo discovered he was accused of a civil cause of action of alienation of affections. (This action was abolished in Vermont in 1973.) The substance of the claim was usually that a person had improperly alienated the affections of a spouse. In almost all cases it also included a count of "criminal conversation."

Criminal conversation was no more than sexual intercourse with a married person. In the 1960s, adultery was still a felony in Vermont, and Vermont had the so-called "Blanket Act" on its statutes. This act was designed to bring people to justice even if actual intercourse was not provable. Thus, people seemingly having an inclination and being found in suggestive circumstances, i.e., under a blanket, were presumed to have engaged in criminal conversation.

What was interesting about the Durocher case was that there was no count of criminal conversation. Leo had simply written a letter to Anna Morin, Carolyn's mother, saying, "Why don't you leave the ornery bastard and come live with us?" René found the letter, and it formed the basis for an allegation of an improper invasion by Leo of the marital relationship of René and Anna, attempting to alienate her affections from her husband.

The next day Leo was released on $50,000 bail, after several of the more prominent citizens of the town of Middlebury agreed to borrow the amount from the National Bank of Middlebury. Each individual carried a potential personal liability of $10,000.

Leo was then free to return to California. Before leaving, however, he retained the services of Conley & Foote. Jack Conley, an ardent baseball fan, was excited about representing Leo "the Lip" Durocher. However, the opportunity fell to his partner, Ralph Foote, who was the lieutenant governor of the state. Jack had to watch the trial from the coaching box.

The trial was scheduled for the week of July 7th, only five months after the case was filed. There was serious concern among the guarantors at the National Bank that Leo might not return to Vermont for the proceedings, and that his bail would be forfeited for the benefit of the plaintiff—all at the cost of the five Middlebury businessmen who had posted it. Eventually, after pleas and threats by the bail posters, Leo Durocher appeared in Middlebury for trial.

Judge Natt Divoll, Jr., presided over the proceedings at the Addison County Courthouse. Gerard Trudeau, the plaintiff's attorney, called Leo to the stand as his first witness. The jurors leaned forward in their cane chairs, their curiosity piqued as Leo walked to the witness box and was sworn in. After the preliminaries of his examination, Trudeau took a baseball from his briefcase, tossed it to Leo on the stand, and asked him to sign it so the jury would have a chance to compare Leo's signature on the baseball with the signature on the letter that was the basis for the case itself. It was not the only baseball Leo autographed on his trip to Middlebury, but it was the only one offered as an exhibit.

The trial lasted for five days. Somewhere in Middlebury there was a cocktail party every evening during the course of the trial. Night after night, Leo was the star guest. It seems that virtually everybody was invited to these parties, including the judge, the side judges, and defense counsel. The only exclusions were those who were blatantly sympathetic to the plaintiff, René Morin, or his counsel, Gerard Trudeau.

The trial resulted in a verdict vindicating the defendant, and Leo went happily back to California, I am sure shaking his head over what had happened in Vermont. One might think that this is the end of the story, but, alas, Leo did not want to pay his legal bills. Conley & Foote had to threaten suit in California to collect those obligations. René Morin decided he did not want to pay his legal bills either, and he was sued in the Addison County Court for collection of Trudeau's legal fees.

2. A Glimpse of the Old Addison County Courthouse

In 1960 there were eight lawyers practicing in Middlebury. Charles Adams had an office in the Addison County Courthouse, and he did mostly probate and real estate work. Bill Burrage, whose office was in the Masonic Building next to the Courthouse, had a practice which was quite general and included some litigation. At the time, he was counsel to the Town of Middlebury. He later became Municipal Judge. The law firm of Conley, Foote & Underwood had just broken up, with Wynn Underwood having started his own practice in 1959. Ralph Foote and Jack Conley formed the firm Conley & Foote, which continues today even after Jack Conley's death in 1971.

Gerard Trudeau, a Middlebury native (and the nephew of three-star-general Arthur Trudeau who retired as Chief of Army Research

& Development), opened a solo practice in 1957. Trudeau brought to the community a more sophisticated approach to practice in terms of attempting to put legal fees on a professional basis. He had worked as an electrical journeyman and pole climber for F.A. Tucker, a Middlebury company that built electric pole lines all over the northeastern United States and eastern Canada, and then had worked with Ryan, Smith & Carbine in Rutland. His philosophy was that lawyers should make as much money as pole climbers.

In addition to these folks, there were two other lawyers in Middlebury, a father and son non-team. Wayne C. Bosworth had an office in the Battell Block, overlooking Merchants Row. His son, Theodore Bosworth, maintained a separate practice at a desk at the other end of the same large room. Wayne Bosworth had been a Rhodes Scholar, was the Reporter of the Decisions for the Vermont Supreme Court until he turned that job over to his son in 1955, and was the only lawyer in Middlebury to have an "A" rating in *Martindale-Hubbell*, the national law directory. Nonetheless, Wayne had acquired a reputation over the years as being somewhat crafty, to put it politely.

In 1961, Tom Lynch, who was then General Counsel for the Rutland Railroad, left that post and went into partnership with Wynn Underwood. They were later joined by Chester Ketcham, and the firm became Underwood, Lynch & Ketcham. The state's attorney in 1960 was Theodore Murin. Ted practiced out of his home in Addison.

Forest Rose, Sam Fishman, and Sam Wagstaff maintained practices in Vergennes, fourteen miles to the north. Sam Fishman was the municipal judge. Sam was also a state senator, having been nominated on both the Republican and Democratic tickets. His family's department store in Vergennes was and still is a landmark in that city.

The only practicing lawyer in Bristol, twelve miles to the northeast, was Ezra Dike. Dike obtained admission to the bar by reading the law in a law office instead of going to law school. He won his first case before the Vermont Supreme Court, arguing his own right to take the Vermont Bar exam.

On November 1, 1960, I was admitted to the Vermont Bar. At the same time, Phyllis Armstrong, a graduate of Middlebury College and Boston University Law School where she was a classmate of F. Lee Bailey, was also admitted. Phyllis was a Middlebury native and was starting her practice as an associate with Conley & Foote.

There was one other frequent traveler to the Addison County

Courthouse, and that was a lawyer from Brandon named Hanford Davis. Hanford's first love was bird hunting and his second was trying lawsuits. He was good at both.

Added to this array of lawyers was the Addison County Courthouse court personnel. George "Punk" Farr was the county clerk. He was from Bristol and he continued in the post of deputy county clerk, actually still running the office long after his "retirement' in 1952. When he died in 1961 at the age of eighty-two, his daughter, Alma Sherwin, who had been the nominal clerk since 1952, took over the actual duties and became a permanent fixture on the Addison County Courthouse scene. She was eventually succeeded by Lois Ann Balch, and then by Kathleen Billings Keeler, who is the clerk today.

None of George Farr's successors can rival him as a character. A few of George's idiosyncrasies are worth recalling. His constant companion was "Lady," a female German shepherd who was affectionate and appeared to be in perpetual heat. When one went into the Clerk's office, one was greeted not only by George but by the dog. Signs of her gender were in evidence as spots of blood all over the wooden floor. The dog was not exactly mangy, but she was in a constant state of shedding. Somehow the dog, the dog hair, and the aroma were not exactly consistent with the professional image one would expect at the county courthouse. Gerry Trudeau had a particular dislike of having to brush the dog hair from his suits, but both George and Gerry managed to survive the relationship, if not always in a harmonious matter.

Another of George's idiosyncrasies was that he had a pet mouse. This was not a little white mouse in a cage, but a country mouse who lived in the courthouse and used to come out of a hole in the wall behind George's desk to drink milk from a saucer that George put out every day. Apparently, the mouse and the dog had a truce, because the dog would watch the mouse and the mouse seemed quite unintimidated. George also had a spittoon, and he almost always had a chew from a plug of Day's Work tobacco tucked away in his cheek. George claimed Day's Work was nothing but "Goddamn alfalfa and molasses," and that it was a shame they didn't make Five Brothers chewing tobacco anymore. He said he had chewed Five Brothers all his life until they raised the price of the plug five cents. This irritated him and he gave up chewing. By the time he arrived at the realization that chewing was more important to him than the additional nickel, Five Brothers had gone out of business and Day's Work was the only plug then available locally on a regular basis.

George's history as an Addison County officer included stints as municipal judge, sheriff, and deputy sheriff. He used to relate stories about the sheriff's department during Prohibition, which indicated that the law-enforcement officers of that time were far from being teetotalers. There was the story about the time George and his deputy brought a prisoner over for a trial in Middlebury from Westport, New York, located on the west shore of Lake Champlain. It was during the wintertime and before the building of the Crown Point Bridge. The three men were driving across the frozen lake in an old Ford. On the way across the lake, George ran into some friends who were ice fishing. As the quality of the fishing at the time was exceeded only by the quality and quantity of the liquid refreshments available, George and his deputy locked the prisoner in an ice shanty. Apparently, it was some two days before they finished their journey from Westport to Middlebury.

Stuart Witherell was the probate judge. His office was located on the first floor in the northwest corner of the courthouse building. Stuart was not a lawyer. That did not seem to hinder him from making legal decisions. Indeed, in Vermont probate judges need not be lawyers. On one occasion a question arose as to the jurisdiction of the matter pending, and a party asked whether the probate court had authority to hear the matter in the first place. Stuart's response was typical: "I'm not exactly sure what this jurisdiction question is all about. Let's just hear the facts and make a decision." I expect Stewart is remembered as much for his contribution as the operator of his weather station in Cornwall as for his actions as a jurist.

Addison County side judges in 1960 were Leon Bushey from Monkton and John Dewitt from Shoreham. Side judges, or assistant judges as they are sometimes called, are an institution that traces back to the time when Vermont was an independent republic. The Republic of Vermont, which adopted its constitution in 1777 (Vermont did not become a state until 1791, the fourteenth), based its constitution on the Pennsylvania model. The Pennsylvania Constitution has its roots in the Magna Carta itself. Following this tradition, the Vermont Constitution declares the rights to which the citizens are entitled and maintains that it is the government's responsibility to provide those rights. This formula departs from the United States Constitution, which is designed to prevent government from taking away from the citizens' rights.

In the days of the Republic of Vermont, and later, in the early days of the State of Vermont, the underlying law adopted by the resident pioneers was the English common law. Since almost all the lawyers at that time were English-trained, the founders were presented with the dilemma of needing the English-based law for purpose of governance, and at the same time distrusting the English-trained lawyers. These lawyers were the same people who represented the political establishment against whom they had been fighting in the recent war for independence.

The office of assistant judge arose in an attempt to balance these competing values. Each county was to elect two persons, almost universally laypersons, who would then sit on the bench with the superior judge, who was a lawyer. The judges' votes carried equal weight, and thus the ultimate power to make decisions remained with the elected representatives of the community. As a practical matter, the side judges also brought from the community to the bench general information which the superior judge did not have as he (the first female superior judge was appointed in 1989) spent much of his time riding circuit around the state.

Although side judges disappeared from the Pennsylvania court system, in Vermont the side judges escaped the judicial reforms of the early twentieth century. By the time anyone looked again at their role, the populist movement had taken over, and Vermont side judges continue to this day as a major political force. They also serve as County Commissioners, and, as such, levy a county tax to maintain the courthouse and the county jail. There was an attempt to abolish side judges in the 1890s, which was unsuccessful because, as one legislator commented in the legislative debate, "If we abolish them, who will brush the flies away from the superior judge?"

Almost always the side judges voted with the superior judge. Even though they were not trained as lawyers, side judges had the power to exercise an equal vote against the position of a superior judge on any matter—including legal conclusions. In the 1980s their judicial powers were finally restricted to fact-finding, and they no longer have the power to overrule the superior judges' interpretation of legal issues.

In the summer of 1958, a personal injury arising out of an automobile accident formed the basis for a trial in the Addison County

Court before presiding Judge Harold "Hack" Sylvester. Wynn Underwood, later to become a Vermont Supreme Court justice, represented the plaintiff, and Bernard Leddy, later to become a United States District Court judge, represented the defendant.

The accident occurred when two automobiles, going in opposite directions, collided head-on on a back road in Bridport. It was winter, the wind was blowing, and a snow squall caused a complete whiteout. Vermont law of negligence at the time incorporated the doctrine of contributory negligence. That meant that in an accident, if the driver of a car was found one percent negligent and the other driver ninety-nine percent negligent, the driver of the first vehicle could not collect against the other because the first driver had contributed to the accident—albeit in a minor way. (This rather harsh doctrine was replaced by a comparative standard in 1969, according to which the jury can compare one driver's negligence against the other driver's.)

At the conclusion of the plaintiff's case and outside the hearing of the jury, Leddy made a motion for the court consisting of Judge Sylvester and Side Judge Bushey (Side Judge Dewitt was ill and was not sitting) to direct the jury to reach a verdict for the defendant. He contended that no reasonable juror could find that the accident was caused solely by the conduct of the defendant. Judge Bushey and Judge Sylvester retired to chambers to take the motion under advisement. If took an unusually long time before they reappeared.

When they came back on the bench, Judge Sylvester, obviously frustrated, made a record that the motion was denied by a one-one vote. He said that he personally would have granted it, but that the older and wiser judge, Bushey, had forced a tie, which had the legal result of denying the motion. The jury took the case and brought back a reasonably generous award for the plaintiff. Judge Bushey always took the jury's verdict for the plaintiff as proof of the wisdom of his legal position, and he carried that belief with him throughout the remaining years he served as assistant judge.

In the summer of 1960 I was fresh out of law school, twenty-two years old, newly married, and working as an unpaid law clerk for Wynn Underwood. I decided to run for state's attorney of Addison County, which then paid the annual sum of $2,000, plus a $400 expense allowance which went toward office supplies and secretarial help. Compensation included eight cents per mile for use of a personal car and reimbursement for meals eaten when away from the county seat on official business. The incumbent, Theodore Murin, had announced for reelection. Roger Bartels, a lawyer, who lived in Goshen but did not have an active practice, also decided to run for state's attorney.

Over the course of the summer, my wife Joann and I mounted a door-to-door campaign. Our goal was to visit every house in the county. I estimate that I actually knocked on eighty percent of the residences in the county. During the day I hit the more rural areas and attempted to talk to the farmers. If no one was home, I simply left a small business card which said "Peter F. Langrock for State's Attorney of Addison County." Starting around five o'clock, Joann and I would go through the various villages door-to-door to ask for support of my candidacy.

I learned a lot about politics that summer. Most Vermonters took the position that if they shook your hand it signified some sort of a commitment to vote for you. I learned on occasion offering my hand for a handshake didn't mean the gesture would be reciprocated. I also learned that when you approached a farmer across the field, you could never expect to be met halfway. But once you crossed the whole field and greeted them personally, they were more than friendly and appreciative of the trouble you took in going to meet them.

On September 19, 1960, all the candidates gathered at the Addison County Courthouse to wait for the towns to call in their individual tallies. Orwell was the first town to call in. I carried Orwell by a two-to-one margin over the incumbent, Theodore Murin, and by a seven-to-one margin over Roger Bartels. That pattern held true for most of the night: with the exception of Addison and Goshen, I carried every town in the county. As there were no candidates in the Democratic primary, I won that nomination as well, on write-ins, which left the general election to be little more than a formality. I will never forget that as the results of the primary became obvious, Ted Murin's wife, Ruby, who later became a good friend, came to me and said, "Well, now that you have got it, I hope you know what to do with it." Her concerns were not unfounded.

Shortly after the general election in November, Ted, who had been having some health problems, decided he would resign. Before assuming the position in my own right on February 1 of 1961, I was appointed by then–Governor and later U.S. Senator Bob Stafford to fill the remainder of Murin's term.

In November of 1960 I made my first court appearance as

state's attorney in the Addison County Courthouse. Municipal court was held on Saturday mornings. I don't know whether this was a convenience for those who were called into court, or if it was a convenience for Judge Fishman, who between his law practice, the legislature, and his store, had a busy five days during the week. In any case, I dressed in my best brown sharkskin three-piece suit and sat at the prosecutor's table.

The very first case I presented was a charge of exceeding the speed limit. In 1960 there was no such thing as a traffic offense. All traffic cases were treated the same as any other misdemeanor case, and all of them required the charging document, an "information" to be signed by the state's attorney. The scene took place in the small courtroom on the first floor, south side, of the courthouse, with the door to the courtroom opening into the center hall left open. The gentleman (whose name I forget), had the good grace to plead guilty, which allowed me to have a perfect one-to-nothing record. Judge Fishman looked down over the bench and said to me, "Mr. State's Attorney, do you have a recommendation as to sentence?" I stood up and placed my hands on my lapels as I had seen other attorneys do, both in real life and in the movies, and said, "Yes, your Honor, I recommend a fine of fifteen dollars." I had no sooner said those words than Jack Conley walking down the hallway of the courthouse said in a loud stage whisper, "Thinks he's a Goddamn Tom Dewey, he does." He said it just loud enough for me to hear, and the hair on the back of my neck started to curl, and my blood pressure must have gone up fifty points. I couldn't wait to get the court session over so I could confront Jack personally with regard to that comment.

There were four or five other defendants and another fifteen or twenty minutes went by before I was released from my responsibilities in court. I immediately ran out of the courthouse—and I do mean ran—to the offices of Conley & Foote. (These had been the former town clerk's offices and were located in the basement area of what had been the old town hall offices, and is now the Knights of Columbus Building.) I walked into the office and asked the secretary if I could see Jack Conley. He heard me, and hollered, "Come on in." As I entered his office, I said, "Jack, if you ever have anything to say to me, say it to my face." He responded, "All right, sit down." I sat down. He went on, "I just want to ask you one question. Who is going to run your office, you or the police?" I stated indignantly, "I am." He looked at me, smiled, and said, "Just remember that."

That was one of the four or five most important defining moments of my legal career. Then and there I made a commitment that I was the person entrusted by the Vermont Constitution to make decisions about the prosecution of the citizens. This was not a decision to be made by the police, nor was I merely the attorney for the police or for the state's investigatory forces. For the almost five years I served as Addison County state's attorney, I tried to fulfill the pledge I made to Jack Conley. A significant portion of what little success I may have had as state's attorney was due directly to that confrontation. Conley was right.

Looking back on it, I must admire Jack for his timing. Had he waited a week, my cockiness might well have been such that the answer to Jack's question would not have been as candid, and I would not have felt bound to the extent that I did by the promise I made on my first day in court.

My first jury trial as state's attorney occurred in a case of willful nonsupport that was filed in superior court. There was a serious problem in municipal court: a backlog of cases that were not being tried. Judge Fishman, for the most part, avoided having trials because they were time-consuming for a part-time judge. Thus for purposes of expedience this case was brought to the superior court. The superior court had a smaller docket, concurrent jurisdiction with the district court on all matters, and full-time judges.

Henry O'Kane was the defendant, and the overseer of the poor of the town of Orwell was the complainant. In 1960 there was no statewide welfare system. Relief for the poor was meted out through an overseer of the poor who was elected in each town. The help the poor received was from the general fund of the town, the budget for which was approved at each town meeting held annually on the first Tuesday of March. A review of the Vermont Reports for 1960 and previous years indicates many cases involving towns fighting over who was financially responsible for indigent individuals who moved from one town to another. This issue had a jurisprudence all of its own.

Thelma Lilly, the overseer, came to me with the factual background that Henry O'Kane had eleven children. She said that O'Kane was living in a tenant house in Orwell and was just a lazy no-good who refused to accept work even when it was offered to him. The town gave him substantial support to ensure that the family did not starve. The overseer presented evidence that on the previous Christmas Eve, O'Kane had found some work, received his paycheck, and then had gone out and drunk up his entire pay, while there were no presents for the children and no food on the table.

I signed an information charging O'Kane, and he was arrested on a Thursday. He could not make the cash bail that was set in the case. Judge William Hill, the presiding judge in superior court, indicated that while he thought cash bail was appropriate, he did not think Mr. O'Kane should spend time in jail without being tried. Judge Hill set a jury trial for the following Monday. In today's procedural morass, it is hard to believe that a case could move from investigation, to arrest, to a full-blown jury trial in a matter of three working days. It did happen. Henry O'Kane was represented by Phyllis Armstrong. This was to be the first test of the two new kids on the block.

AN ASIDE

There were thirteen people taking the bar exam in 1960 and Phyllis and I were among the eleven who passed. The bar exam was given in the State Senate chambers at the Capitol, in Montpelier. The first two days consisted of written essay-type answers to questions that covered a variety of subjects of Vermont law. The third day was orals. The oral examination for each individual was relatively short. I remember my examiners were Pearly Feen, the grand old man of the bar, and Jim Oakes, who later went on to become attorney general of the state and finally chief judge of the United States Court of Appeals for the Second Circuit. It was rumored that the orals were used only to sort out whether somebody who was on the margin on the written exams should be admitted or sent back for another year's study. In the early afternoon of the third day, a member of the Board of Bar Examiners told us all to go out to have a beer and be back at about 3:30. At 3:30 all thirteen duly assembled in the anteroom of the House and Senate chambers. One of the bar examiners came and asked two people to come with him. Shortly thereafter we saw those two individuals going down the back stairs to the first floor. At that point, all the bar examiners came into the waiting area and congratulated us on passing the bar and welcomed us to the profession.

While this experience seems a far cry from the tensions engendered by today's bar exams, one must put it in perspective. There were fewer than three hundred practicing lawyers in Vermont at the time, and everybody knew virtually every-body else. The relationship among lawyers was usually cordial, and everybody knew who the few bad apples were that could not be trusted. A lawyer's word or handshake was a bond.

Friday's interview of Mrs. O'Kane verified the facts that the overseer of the court had reported. She agreed to cooperate with the prosecution and would testify in court. On Monday morning she arrived in court with her youngest child, still an infant in her arms. I met her in the hallway of the courthouse on the second floor and went over her upcoming testimony with her. I then suggested that the court officer hold her baby while she testified. She said in no way would she allow the court officer to hold the child and either she was going to hold the child or she would not take the stand. I told her I was sure the defense would object to her taking the stand in a nonsupport case holding the baby in her arms. The only alternative acceptable to her was to have her husband hold the child. As this was my first trial and the first test of two of the newest admittees to the bar, the attention of the entire bar of the county and, of course, of Colonel Slater, publisher of the *Addison County Independent* news-paper, was upon us. I had three choices: dismiss the case, attempt by some process to force the child from the arms of its mother, or allow the defendant to hold the child. The least of the evils was the third choice.

Imagine this picture: The State's Attorney addressing the court, "My first witness is Mrs. Henry O'Kane." Sitting on the bench is Judge Hill, flanked by the two side judges. Facing the bench to the left is the county clerk, George Farr. To the right of the bench are the jury and Mrs. Jones, the court reporter. In what was then a sec-ond jury box on the left side of the court, there sat several members of the bar and a representative of the Fourth Estate, a reporter from the *Addison County Independent*. Through the swinging doors at the back of the courtroom comes Mrs. Henry O'Kane carrying infant O'Kane in her arms. As she walks up the alleyway in front of the jury box moving towards the witness stand, she leans over and hands the baby to her husband, who is sitting next to his attorney, Phyllis Armstrong, at the table immediately behind the prosecutor's table. (In 1960 the prosecution sat at a table that was closest to the bench. Defense counsel was seated at an identical table immediately behind the prosecution.)

Henry O'Kane took the child and started goo-gooing her and

throwing her up in the air over his head. Obviously enjoying this, the child gurgled and smiled. Mrs. O'Kane raised her right hand and was sworn to tell the truth and then sat down in the witness box. I cleared my throat, and for the first time ever I asked a question of a witness: "Could you please state your full name for the record?" At this point Mrs. O'Kane looked at me with a tearful face, and in a high-pitched voice pleaded, "Please don't send my husband to jail." It was apparent to all that my nascent career as a trial lawyer had hit an immediate low. My only hope was to survive long enough for it to improve. I nervously proceeded to try to bring out the facts from the witnesses when Mrs. Jones, the court reporter, who used the traditional yellow lead pencils to take down the testimony on lined sheets of paper in her Gregg shorthand, turned and threw a pencil directly at me with the admonition, "Will you slow down!" Thankfully, the pencil missed, but the jury as well as the assembly of lawyers on the other side of the courtroom were openly amused.

During the course of the trial, Phyllis Armstrong, using the demonstrative techniques she learned in her Boston University Law School trial-practice course, brought out a blackboard and established the aid given to this family of thirteen over the course of the year had amounted to something less than three dollars per day. The jury concluded this was not a sufficient sum taken from the town's general fund to justify a conviction of willful nonsupport, and they brought back a verdict of not guilty. I think they were right.

When I took over the state's attorney's office, the backlog was about three hundred cases, ranging from a handful of serious felonies to a lot of traffic violations. Tom Debevoise, attorney general for the state, came down to Middlebury to discuss how I should proceed to get that docket under control. I then learned the first rudiments of plea negotiations.

Tom had run for state's attorney of Windsor County in 1958 and had been defeated. He then took the position as deputy attorney general. Attorney General was a two-person office back in those days, and when the attorney general resigned, Tom took over as attorney general. Tom's father, a man of heroic proportions in the early days of the Lawyers' Committee for Civil Rights, was the founding partner of Debevoise & Plimpton, the prestigious New York City law firm. After leaving the attorney general's office, Tom practiced in both Vermont and Washington. He returned to Vermont full-time in 1974 to serve as Dean of the fledgling Vermont Law School, located in the small town of South Royalton.

Among the pending cases were three speeding charges all being defended by the firm of Conley & Foote. We could not reach an agreement—I expect because Jack Conley wanted Phyllis Armstrong to have some early jury-trial experience and the stakes were not too high to allow a beginning lawyer to try them. In fairness to the defendants in those speeding cases, there was no point system back then and the commissioner of motor vehicles had a rather arbitrary authority by which he could suspend licenses on a first conviction of speeding, and often did.

A jury panel was summoned for a Saturday morning in the municipal court. We started off at 8:30 a.m. with Judge Fishman on the bench, myself prosecuting, and my classmate at the bar, Phyllis Armstrong, defending all three cases.

As things got underway that December Saturday morning, Phyllis's mentor and employer, Jack Conley, was standing in the wings. In the first case, we proceeded to draw the jury, make the opening statements, put the evidence on, argue the case, hear the judge make his charge to the jury, wait for the jury's deliberations, and then take the jury's verdict. The jury was out for about ten minutes and brought back a verdict of guilty. A sentence of a small fine was imposed.

The same panel of jurors was reassembled, another jury was selected, and we proceeded to try the second case. Again we went through the full formalities of a trial, from opening statements to the presentation of evidence, arguments, closing, and jury charge. This time the jury was out for about half an hour and then brought back another verdict of guilty. Again, a sentence of a small fine was imposed.

We started on the third complete jury trial of the day. Members of the bar were coming in and out of the courtroom, curious to see the two young lawyers mixing it up before a jury. In this case, after the completion of the evidence, arguments, and the court's charge, the jury deliberated for over an hour. The jury deliberations extended into the second hour, which presented a problem as all the lawyers and all the police officers involved were anxious to go to the American Legion Hall where their help was required to put on the annual "cops and robbers" dinner. Finally the jury came back, and once again they announced a verdict of guilty. Two jurors leaving the courthouse were overheard saying, "It's too bad that we had to bring in a conviction in the last case. It would have been nice for Miss Armstrong to have a win."

One can be assured that the convictions were brought about by the fact that the three people were simply speeding, and not by any legal acumen of the State's Attorney.

Do three complete jury trials on the same day, a Saturday, with the same judge and counsel, qualify for the *Guinness Book of Records?*

In the 1960s I was retained in three other jury cases that I group together because they establish my record with opposing counsel Hanford Davis, a gifted trial lawyer. After the 1959 trial of Bucky Dragon I had the opportunity to try three jury cases against Hamp Davis. Hamp won them all.

The first of these came about when a client of Hamp's, one "Doc" Mitchell, was seen attempting to spot wild deer by a game warden named Leroy Aldrich. After seeing the car headlights go around a field, Aldrich turned on his red-flashing light and then proceeded to chase the vehicle down Route 116 on to Quarry Road and toward Middlebury. Aldrich's lights were flashing, his siren was sounding, and finally Doc pulled over. As the deer-spotlighting case was weak, he was charged with careless and negligent operation of a motor vehicle. Doc plead not guilty and the case went to a jury trial before the Honorable Natt Divoll, Jr.

Aldrich took the stand and he told his story. Several occupants of houses along Route 116 and Quarry Road testified they had seen the lights flashing and heard the siren. The state rested its case. Hamp made a motion for a directed verdict of acquittal, saying that the state's game warden had not directly identified the defendant as the driver of the car, nor had he offered evidence that the defendant was the sole occupant of the car. I moved to reopen the evidence, but Judge Divoll looked at me, smiled patronizingly, granted the motion, dismissed the jury, and suggested that the next time I should be more careful and prepare an outline of all the elements of the charge. The fact that Judge Divoll wanted to take the afternoon off to go duck hunting, I'm sure, had nothing to do with his decision.

The next case Hamp defended was the usury prosecution of Sam Emilo mentioned earlier.

The third case is connected with the Addison County Courthouse because the characters of the story were often there, and it's worth telling because it was typical of some cases that went to trial in the 1960s. The plaintiff—this time represented by me—was none other than the same Doc Mitchell.

Doc made his living buying and selling everything from live buf-

faloes to cows, from goats and horses to antiques. He had entered a
deer pool run by his brother, Robert Mitchell, who ran a sporting
goods store in Brandon. Prior to deer season, hunters in Brandon
and surrounding towns paid a small fee to enter Robert Mitchell's
deer pool. The person who shot the largest buck was awarded a
brand-new deer rifle, a .300 Savage, and whoever shot the smallest
buck received a .22 caliber rifle as the consolation prize.

Shortly after the opening hour on the first morning of deer season, Doc arrived with a large, twelve-point buck that some claimed
was already stiff with rigor mortis. This would suggest that the deer
had been shot sometime prior to the opening of deer season, perhaps sometime around midnight the night before. At almost 200
pounds it was the heaviest deer reported—as well as the first. The
Mitchell brothers, Doc and Bob, did not get along well, and Doc's
buck did not help the situation. The crowning blow, however, was
when Doc's son Beaver reported a small deer, which placed him in
the lead for the consolation prize. This was too much for brother
Bob. Bob found a hunter in Rochester who had shot a small buck.
He helped him cut all the meat off the ribs, sew the skin back onto
the ribs, and then weigh it in. This knocked out Beaver's claim for
the .22, but Doc still had the lead in the quest for the deer rifle. At
the close of the season, no one had brought in a bigger deer.
Concerned about accusations of nepotism despite the well-known
animosity between the brothers, and fueled by skepticism over how
Doc's deer had been taken, Bob refused to pay off the pool or award
the rifle to Doc. Bob further claimed that the deer had been left in
water overnight in order for the hollow deer hairs to soak up water
and take on additional weight. He also claimed that Doc had put a
lead pipe in the deer's throat to enhance its weight.

Doc hired me to resolve the dispute. We brought suit in the
Rutland District Court for the value of the rifle (about $300), which
Doc claimed to have rightfully won. Doc's brother Bob retained
Hamp Davis, and we went to a jury trial before Municipal Judge
Richard Sullivan. Among the witnesses Hamp called for the defense
was a game warden, Arnold Magoon, who testified that in fact he
was present when the deer was skinned, and that a large pool of
water had accumulated when the pelt dropped to the floor. On
cross-examination Magoon admitted that he had not seen any sign
of a lead pipe in the deer's throat. The jury deliberated for about an
hour before they finally decided in favor of Bob, letting both individuals stay in the status quo. Doc did not get his gun, and I had an

0-3 record with Hamp. That record stood for twenty years (Hamp died in 1983.)

Doc's farm was known as the poor farm. During the first half of the twentieth century, before there was any welfare safety net, towns owned and maintained farms which were designated as poor farms. People who were unable to find work, couldn't work, or were simply destitute, were housed there at the expense of the town. In exchange, they were expected to work on the farm to reduce the cost to the towns of the maintenance of the operation.

Middlebury's poor farm was located on the northwest corner of the intersection between Route 7 and the East Middlebury River. The bridge that crosses the river at that point has always been known as the "Poor Farm Bridge." The town poor farm itself was closed decades ago and sold into private hands to increase the town tax base. This location was Doc's principal point of trading. He had converted the large garage building into an antique shop, and the barns in back of the house were used to stable the horses, cows, goats, and other animals that he was constantly buying and selling. He often used the front porch of the house as a platform for auctions of every imaginable sort.

On one occasion, the Salisbury Volunteer Fire Department decided to have an auction, and Doc agreed to hold it at his place. The fire department gathered up all sorts of donations, from farm implements to antiques, advertised the event, and drew a good crowd. Doc asked me to assist as an auctioneer, more for the fun of it than on account of my auctioneering abilities. Well into the auction I spelled Doc for a while, using an imperfect sing-song that I had picked up from listening to auctioneers over the years. I started to get a little hoarse. Doc handed me a can of orange soda and said, "Take a drink of this, it'll be good for your throat." Contrary to my expectation, the can did not contain pure orange soda by any means. The first half of the can of orange soda had been dumped on the ground and replaced with vodka. This improved both my throat and my self-perceived auctioneering prowess.

On one of his trading forays into the Midwest, Doc Mitchell attended an auction where they were selling buffalo. He decided it would be a profitable venture for him to buy several of the animals at the auction in South Dakota and bring them back to Vermont, where he could turn them over for a profit. As it turned out, Doc was able to dispose of all the buffalo en route from South Dakota to his farm, with the exception of one young bull calf.

Upon arriving home with the young buffalo bull, Doc placed him in the barn with a door open so the calf would have access to a well-fenced paddock. A local game warden driving by noticed the animal in the paddock and recognized it immediately as an American Bison. As far as he was concerned, an American Bison was a wild animal. He asked Doc whether he had a permit to keep the animal. Doc replied quite candidly that he hadn't, that he'd recently bought the animal in South Dakota and had brought it home. The game warden responded that as this was a wild animal, and since Doc didn't have a permit, he had a duty to turn it loose. Legal technicalities aside, Doc recognized that this would be an insane thing to do, as the animal would undoubtedly wander onto a road and not only get itself killed, but would most probably injure or kill a person at the same time. Upon receiving a criminal citation for harboring a wild animal without a permit, Doc sought the help of my partner, Jon Stahl. Jon contacted the Commissioner of Fish and Game, and eventually obtained a permit for Doc to keep the buffalo in an enclosed area, so the criminal case was dismissed. Doc soon traded the animal at a much smaller profit than he had expected, and he had to pay his attorney's fees to boot.

3. The Note Shavers

In 1961 the dean of the Addison County Bar was Wayne C. Bosworth. Throughout my clerkship with the firm of Conley, Foote & Underwood, and then with Wynn Underwood's solo practice, I was often told that Wayne—the senior member of the Addison County Bar—was not to be trusted. As Wayne seldom appeared on behalf of a defendant in a criminal case, I had very few dealings with him initially. In the late fall of 1961, all of this changed.

In 1961, Vermont had on its books a usury law which provided that anyone who charged interest in excess of six percent per annum was guilty of a misdemeanor. The low legal interest rates caused the banks to be very cautious in their lending policies.

In an attempt to get around the tight banking procedures, a system called note shaving developed. There was a group of about half a dozen men in Addison County who engaged in this practice. The way a note shaver worked is this: say you arranged to borrow $500 from him. He had you sign a note for $700, plus the going rate of interest, and then he endorsed the note over to a bank, received the face amount of the loan from the bank, and gave you the $500, pocketing the $200 difference. You had to make the payments to the bank to pay off the full face value of $700. If you defaulted, the bank looked to the note shaver for payment, and then that note shaver came after you. Cash was a scarce commodity in Vermont in the early 1960s, and note shavers did a thriving business.

There were many variations on this theme, all of which violated the usury laws. As state's attorney, I launched an investigation into these matters. During the course of the investigation, I found that the great bulk of the notes were discounted at the Caledonia National Bank, located in Danville, Vermont. Based upon the preliminary investigation, I obtained a search warrant. A uniformed state police officer and I went off to Danville with warrant in hand, the warrant calling for a search of the bank for various documents which would constitute evidence of a usury scheme. Officer Rodney Mott, one of only four state troopers assigned to Addison County at the time, worked on the investigation with me.

Danville is a rural community with a population of less than two thousand located in northeastern Vermont, about ten miles west of St. Johnsbury. On the edge of the town green stands the bank building itself. Upon entering the building you would think you were on a movie set, for, instead of the usual informal tellers' windows and counter, sophisticated bullet-proof glass shields separate the customer area from the bank offices, and on the top of the shields are small rolls of sharp-edged barbed wire—miniatures of what you might see on fences surrounding prisons. Each teller station had a revolving window for the exchange of currency and checks and was designed so that there was never any direct contact between the customer and the teller. This entire paraphernalia was installed in the 1930s as the then state-of-the-art security system, in response to a robbery at the bank. The Caledonia National Bank was said to be the first national bank robbed subsequent to Congress passing the federal bank-robbery statutes. The prosecution and defense of that robbery involved two of Vermont's giants at the bar: Deane C. Davis, who was Governor of Vermont from 1968 to 1972; and Sterry Waterman, who became the second Vermonter ever to serve on the United States Court of Appeals for the Second Circuit.

Upon presentation of the warrant, we were ushered into the office of Sheldon Houghton, the bank manager. We asked Houghton for his cooperation and he requested permission to first call his attorney, Arthur Graves. Arthur Graves was the senior states-man of the Caledonia County Bar. He had been practicing long enough so that his picture as a young man was included in the poster-size photograph of the entire Vermont Bar of 1911. Arthur promised on the phone that if we would forgo the use of the search warrant, he would see that his clients honored a subpoena for all rel-evant documents. Taking him at his word, we left the bank without going through the bank records, and with a clear understanding that all the documents that had been sought under the search warrant would be turned over pursuant to a subpoena.

Years later, Joseph Rattigan of Rutland, who was the United States Attorney for Vermont at the time of the attempted search, told me that as a result of our appearance at the bank, Arthur Graves had filed a complaint with his office charging State Police Officer Mott and me with attempted armed bank robbery in our effort to execute the search warrant, as Mott was armed with his standard issue police revolver. At the time, Rattigan told Graves that he thought the charge was ridiculous, and he only related the story to me later as what was, in his mind, a humorous incident. However, the fact that Graves actually filed such a charge gives an inkling of the approach the established bar took to a young upstart prosecutor who was going to examine the traditions of note shaving and relat-ed financial matters. These illegal practices were supported by some members of the bar who prepared the paperwork and who on occa-sion participated directly as principals.

During the course of this investigation, it appeared that a dairy farmer in Waltham had been deceived by a member of the bar. The Farnsworth farm was one of the largest and best farms in Addison County, with a stanchion barn holding two hundred cows and more than seven hundred acres of cropland. The Federal Land Bank held a first mortgage in the amount of $25,000 and a cattle dealer by the name of Cochrane, from Barre, held a second mortgage in the amount of $10,000. Farnsworth had fallen behind in his payments to the federal Land Bank, and the bank had commenced a foreclo-sure proceeding. Under Vermont law, once foreclosure was started, the mortgagor was given the option of paying the full balance or los-ing the entire farm. Under this doctrine of so-called strict foreclosure, the mortgagor had six months to raise the money and redeem his mortgage, or the mortgagee would take title to the property pursuant to a court decree. Whatever equity there might be in the property would then belong to the mortgagee. The Federal Land Bank had in fact started a foreclosure in the early part of 1961 and was represented by Frederick "Ted" Bosworth, Wayne Bosworth's son.

Wayne and his son, Ted, claimed to maintain separate practices, despite the fact they had desks in the same room. In September, the six-month redemption period was running out, and Farnsworth came to Ted Bosworth's office to see if there was any way he could work things out and save his farm. Ted referred him across the room to his father, who there hatched out the following plan: Farnsworth would deed the property to Samuel Emilo, one of the note shavers. Sam would then mortgage the property to the Addison County Trust Company (later merged into the Chittenden Trust Company) to obtain the $25,000 to pay off the first mortgage. The Addison County Trust Company was ready to loan this money, based not just on the security of the farm, but upon an agreement by Wayne Bosworth and his wife to endorse the note. The bank would look to Wayne to make sure the payments were current. Emilo was to supply the $10,000 to pay off the second mortgage. Emilo was to execute an option back to Farnsworth to allow him to repurchase his farm from Sam upon repayment of all the monies borrowed, all expenses, all interest accrued, and an additional $1,000 per month for the time Sam held the farm. This option would expire in six months, at which point Emilo would be the sole owner of the farm and free to sell it on the open market.

The real value of the farm was two to three times the total of the mortgages, and thus if the six month period went by without Farnsworth exercising his option, there were large sums of money to be made. Sam and the two Bosworths entered into a private agreement to share the profits equally among the three of them. If Farnsworth was actually able to raise the monies to repurchase the property from some other source, they would still have profits of $1,000 per month for the time it took Farnsworth to arrange other financing. The papers were styled in the form of a purchase-and-sale with a buy-back option. In reality, they were a loan with an interest rate of approximately 35 percent per annum. If you calculate the return Sam and the Bosworths were getting for the actual money they had invested from their own pockets, an interest rate of infinitely higher percentage would be applicable. The security was so great they had virtually no risk at all.

After talking to Farnsworth and reviewing the paperwork, but before deciding to prosecute, I went to talk to Wynn Underwood, my mentor under whom I had served my clerkship. I told him of the situation, and said I had what I thought was probable cause for a criminal prosecution for usury against the senior member of the bar, Wayne Bosworth. Wynn suggested that Bosworth was a crook and that this was the type of thing he had been doing for years. He went further and told me stories about how Bosworth had put some very good farmers out of business using techniques such as this. He said he thought the prosecution should go forward. After my conversation with Wynn Underwood, I approached the then-presiding judge of the Addison County Court, Harold "Hack" Sylvester, with a request for a grand jury. I was hoping to test my judgment about going forward with a final decision to be made by the twenty-three members of a grand jury. Sylvester looked at me and said, "Peter, you don't need a grand jury. Call an inquest, get the facts you need, and then make up your own mind to go forward or not." I did just that. Wayne was duly arrested to answer to the charge of usury, was released without cash bail, and the matter was appropriately docketed on the court's calendar.

It wasn't long before a motion was made to disqualify me from prosecuting the case, claiming that I had a bias against Wayne Bosworth. Rumors had gotten back to me that people were making bets on how long it would be before I was run out of town by the establishment. Both the arrest of Wayne Bosworth and the motion to disqualify were lead news articles in the *Addison County Independent*.

I became concerned that perhaps I had bitten off more than I could chew, and one day in that frame of mind I walked down-street from my offices at the courthouse to the post office on Main Street. Coming up the street was E. B. Cornwall, a member of the bar, who was then active as a professor at Middlebury College rather than as a practicing lawyer. He stopped me and I wasn't sure what to expect. "Peter, I read in the paper about your prosecution of Bosworth. He has always been a crook, has taken advantage of a lot of farmers, and I am glad you're out to try to do what is right."

E. B. was a man who had been involved in Vermont politics since the Great Depression. He was in his early eighties, had served the state as its first Commissioner of Employment Security, and was a person whom I respected greatly. His few words of encouragement put the entire matter into perspective and gave me a much-increased comfort level.

A few days later Wynn asked me to meet him for lunch. We went down to Lockwood's Restaurant on Merchants Row, and after chatting about some fishing and hunting matters, he started to ask me questions about what I had learned about the Bosworth case during the investigation. After a few minutes of what I perceived to be his pumping me for information, I asked Wynn outright, incredulous, "Are you going to represent Wayne Bosworth?" He said, "Well, he has been in to see me, and I guess I probably will." I stopped discussing the case with him at that point and no longer considered him my mentor. Wynn did go on to represent Wayne. Ted Bosworth, who was also arrested, was represented by Jack Conley. Jack was not surreptitious at all about his representation of Ted. He told me one day, "I'm going to represent Ted. Might as well keep the money in town." Sam Emilo was represented by "Hamp" Davis.

Judge William "Oliver Wendell" Hill was scheduled to hear the motion to disqualify me from prosecuting the case. (The nickname "Oliver Wendell" came at a later time when he was sitting on the Vermont Supreme Court where he was perceived as thinking of himself as a great jurist.) Hill denied the motion and the case went forward. By the time the case came to trial, most of the note shavers had entered into a plea agreement, received a small fine, and were told to go forth and sin no more. This left three cases for trial: Wayne Bosworth, Samuel Emilo, and Ted Bosworth.

Wayne's trial was scheduled first, and by this time Harold "Hack" Sylvester had rotated back into Addison County as the presiding judge. It promised to be a very close trial. The paperwork on its face indicated this was a legitimate transaction where the property had been sold by Farnsworth to Emilo, and Emilo had given a valid option back at a different price. The prosecution as going to have to convince the jury the form of the transaction was merely a sham for a refinancing, and the essence of the transaction was a loan with a usurious interest rate. Representing the state, I put on my case, calling Farnsworth to the stand. He testified that he had heard Wayne and Ted talking about placing the loan with the Addison County Trust Company. He was quite clear in his testimony that he never intended to sell the farm, and in fact had never moved from the farm nor stopped actively farming it. He said the scheme was designed to extend his financing for an additional six months to see if he could find some permanent funding someplace else. After the admission into evidence of the pertinent documents, the state rested, and Wynn Underwood, on behalf of his client, moved to take the case away from the jury by means of a directed verdict of acquittal. Judge Sylvester and the side judges listened to the arguments pro and con carefully, and decided to let the matter go to the jury.

Underwood started his defense. His chief witness was the defendant himself. Wayne testified he was merely the attorney for Sam Emilo and that he had drafted papers according to the wishes of Farnsworth, selling the property to Emilo, but with the understanding there would be an option to repurchase. On cross-examination I asked several questions and then focused in on the option agreement and whether it was the intention of the Farnsworths to actually sell their farm. Sam Emilo was not a farmer but was known as a financier in the community. In reply to one question regarding the effect of Emilo's purchase, Wayne said, "Well, the Farnsworths could always redeem." I got halfway through my next question when I realized that Bosworth had used the word "redeem." Redeem is a term of art that is used in mortgage-foreclosure proceedings and is not used in purchase-and-sale or option agreements. I stopped in mid-question and said, "Did you use the word redeem? Isn't that a word associated with mortgages and foreclosures?" The former Rhodes Scholar in Bosworth came to the front and he said, "The word redeem comes from the Latin to buy back and therefore it is perfectly appropriate in connection with a sale with an option to repurchase." A look at the jury told me that they were not sympathetic to his explanation of the Latin roots of the word "redeem." It just emphasized in their minds that he had inadvertently used a word that was more properly associated with mortgages, loans, and foreclosures.

At the conclusion of the defense, the court charged the jury as to what was the applicable law, and the jury retired to deliberate. About two hours later they returned with a verdict of guilty. The court imposed as the only sentence a fine of $100 and Bosworth announced his intention to take an appeal to the Vermont Supreme Court.

The next day we started trial of the case against Sam. The transaction was the same, but "Hamp" Davis was defense counsel. Emilo was a likable person who had a good sense of humor and seemed to get along well with common folk. At one point during his testimony, he described the facts surrounding his finally taking out a bank loan to cover the second $10,000 mortgage he had paid off. What he was describing was a check-kiting scheme where he had to get some real money in order to prevent his financial lacework of checks from collapsing. He looked at the jury and said, "I had so much paper in the air, I had to find some real money, and that's why we got the loan." Today he probably would be prosecuted for bank fraud, but back then all he got was a laugh from the jury. "Hamp" in his defense took the position that whatever the transaction was, it was designed by Bosworth, and Emilo thought that the transaction was a legitimate sale with a repurchase option and that he had no intention to violate the usury laws. The jury bought this argument and Sam was acquitted.

Eventually, I dismissed the case against Ted Bosworth, as he was only a minor player in this entire matter and I was not at all sure he would be convicted. The back had already been broken of the group of financiers who had been unfairly preying upon people in need of short-term financing.

At the appellate level before the Vermont Supreme Court, Wayne hired John Calhoun to replace Wynn Underwood as his lawyer. John Calhoun was a Middlebury native who had not gone to law school but had read law in Wayne Bosworth's office and, upon passing the bar, first had served as state's attorney of Addison County and then had opened a practice in Barre. In the *Bosworth* appeal, Calhoun argued two major points: (1) that the trial court had erred in failing to disqualify the state's attorney and (2) that the transaction itself was an appropriate one of a sale with an option back and not a loan at a usurious interest rate.

The chief justice at that time was Benjamin N. Hurlburd who had a penchant for the English common law and the decisions of the great English jurist, Lord Mansfield. In preparing the brief, I carefully set out a decision of Lord Mansfield on the question of usury, quoting him. "Where the real truth is a loan of money, the wit of man cannot find a shift to take it out of the statute." I worked hard on the brief and after several drafts finally polished a phrase to my special liking which I inserted into the brief next to the Mansfield quotation. In December of 1963, Justice Hurlburd wrote the opinion for a unanimous court affirming the conviction. It was one of the last opinions he wrote before he died. One of the small ego trips that a lawyer occasionally receives is when the court recognizes a particular phrase or sentence that the lawyer has especially groomed for the situation. Justice Hurlburd did exactly that in the opinion, and after citing the above quotation from Lord Mansfield he wrote, "There is much sense in the state's attorney's argument 'that the same reasons of necessity that force a borrower into the hands of a usurer would prevent the borrower from dictating the form of the papers to be drawn covering the transaction.'"[1]

Interestingly enough, there was never any disciplinary action, even by way of reprimand, taken against Wayne Bosworth by the attorney general's office, which was then in charge of professional discipline. It is also interesting that in his later years Wayne used to consider me the lawyer he trusted most in Middlebury. When he had a perplexing problem he wished to discuss with somebody, he would wander into my office and chat about it. When he reached ninety and decided he was going to retire from the practice of law, his son having predeceased him by several years, he came to me and said he wanted me to have his library, and he set a price on his entire collection of books that was sufficiently low I could not refuse it. After closing his office, in 1980, he was still seen well into his nineties driving around town in his little yellow Volkswagen beetle, a complete menace to all on the road.

During the course of the usury investigations, the name of Euclide Quesnel kept creeping up. At first it appeared he might be another note shaver, but as it turned out he was actually a customer of the note shavers. Euclide, a cattle dealer from town, liked to drive a large Cadillac, wear a ten-gallon hat, smoke a big cigar, and trade cattle. Some of his practices—in trading cattle, as well as in other financial dealings—were questionable. He had often been a client of Wayne Bosworth's, and from time to time he had entered into a variety of transactions with farmers that left him with somewhat of an unsavory reputation.

One day I received a call from a hired man named Robert J. Kemp who was working on a farm in Weybridge. He wanted to come in to talk to me right away. In my state's attorney's office rooms at the back of the courthouse, he unfolded the following tale. That very morning Kemp had received in the mail a canceled note from the Burlington Savings Bank. The note was marked "paid in full" and bore his signature. The only problem was he had never borrowed any money from that bank. In thinking back how this could have happened, he finally pieced it together.

Kemp had been working as a hired man on one of Euclide's farms. Six months earlier Euclide had come in and asked him to sign some papers for Social Security purposes. Unbeknownst to Kemp, Euclide had included a blank note in that sheaf of papers. Kemp signed the papers in blank and then Euclide filled out the note in the amount that he personally wanted to borrow. Euclide then went to the bank, discounted the note, and obtained the funds. Euclide's direct line of credit, which allowed him to borrow in his own name, had run out, but he still had some ability to endorse notes for farmers to whom he had sold cattle. In those transactions the bank would rely upon his endorsement and pay the money to them, charging it against an indirect line of credit rather than treating it as a personal loan. Euclide had portrayed Kemp's note as a cattle note and had taken the proceeds for his personal use. Each month when the bank would send out the notice calling for a payment, Euclide would intercept Kemp's mail and make the payment.

Two weeks earlier, Kemp had quit Quesnel's employ and gone to work for another farmer. When this happened, Euclide promptly went to the bank and paid off the balance on the note. What Euclide didn't expect was that the bank would return the note directly to Kemp and that the post office would, noting Kemp's change of address, forward it directly to him. Euclide did not have an opportunity to intercept the return of the paid note, and Kemp turned it over as evidence of the fraud.

Euclide was arraigned before the Addison Superior Court and Jack Conley came in as defense counsel. The case was scheduled for trial before Judge William Hill. The charge was a felony and alleged that Euclide had obtained something of more than $25 value by means of false pretenses. One of the legal questions involved was how to value what Euclide had obtained. Kemp was not out a single nickel, and one could even argue that his credit record had been improved by the borrowing of money with its timely repayment. Under Vermont law if the value of the property obtained by the fraud was less than $25, it was a misdemeanor. If the value was determined to be more than $25, the fraud was a felony. During the cross-examination of one of Euclide's sons, Bernie Quesnel, I heard Jack and his client in a muffled conversation behind me. I took this opportunity to ask Bernie the question that certainly the use of Mr. Kemp's credit on this note was worth more than $25, wasn't it? Bernie leaped to the bait and jumped in and said, "It certainly was worth more than $25." I'm not sure Jack ever really heard the question and I quickly moved on to another matter. This gave me the evidentiary basis in the record for sustaining a felony conviction. Euclide was convicted, fined $700, and placed on probation, without having to serve any time, despite my request for a jail sentence.

While the matter was on appeal, I would run into Euclide from time to time in the community. We had one very close acquaintance in common—Bill Rule. Bill ran the Flying A service station at the corner of Elm and North Pleasant Streets. One day we were both there getting gas, and Euclide turned to me and said, "Peter, I was really hurt when you asked for a jail sentence. You really didn't want that, did you?" I simply smiled and pointed out that the court handled the matter and it had made the decision on the sentence. A short time later I ran into Euclide again, just after a barn on one of his farms had burned and the insurance company was questioning whether it should pay the loss. Not missing an opportunity, Euclide asked me how much I would charge him to collect the monies that were due him from the insurance company. I replied simply, "Euclide, you know your case is on appeal.² I can't represent you in any matter whatsoever." He smiled ruefully, and I had to give him an "A" for trying.

In later years, Euclide and I became friends. I had known his son Bernie and his other son Louis since we were teenagers together and went to the same summer square dances at Cove Point on Lake Dunmore, just south of Middlebury. Some years later Euclide called me concerning a subpoena he had received from the United States Attorney's Office in Syracuse about certain cattle which had been smuggled into New York from Canada, and which he had supposedly transported from upstate New York, near the alleged smuggling spot, to Vermont. The subpoena at this point was for his records only, and I suggested that he send one of his sons over with the records rather than going himself. Euclide's curiosity prevailed. He declined to follow my advice, and he went to Syracuse with the books.

While he was there, the U.S. Attorney invited him to appear before the federal grand jury, and Euclide—with his best cattle-dealer's bravado, believing that he could talk anybody out of anything—welcomed the opportunity. After his testimony, he was indicted on a felony of conspiring to smuggle cattle. He was also charged with a couple of misdemeanor counts dealing with improper movement of cattle. More importantly he was indicted on four felony counts of committing perjury before the grand jury. A perjury conviction almost always results in a jail sentence.

After the indictments were handed down, I called up the U.S. Attorney, Gus DeBianco, with whom I had been negotiating concerning the turning over of the records, and said, "Gus, why didn't you telephone me before you called Euclide in before the grand jury so that I could have advised him appropriately?" Gus, who was a straight shooter, agreed that maybe a call would have been appropriate and said that he would drop all the perjury counts if my client would plead guilty to the conspiracy count. This meant that Euclide had a chance of escaping a jail sentence.

The day came when Euclide and I journeyed to Albany to enter a plea before U.S. Federal District Judge Foley. Foley was then the last active member of the federal bench appointed by President Harry S. Truman. He was a delightful man, small in physical stature but very large in his sense of humanity. He accepted the plea and ordered a presentence investigation.

When the time came for our return to Albany for sentencing, I was really worried about Euclide. He was just recovering from a heart attack, and despite every device I knew and tried, I was unable to predict whether there was a real chance of his going to jail. I did find out that in the course of the presentence investigation, Euclide told the investigator that he was worth a lot of money and that a fine really wouldn't bother him. Once again, his penchant for braggadocio might get him into trouble.

We were in the main courtroom in the federal building on State Street in Albany when Judge Foley came out to the bench. Euclide was required to stand and face the judge as sentence was imposed. I stood next to him and could see that he was pale and looked quite frightened. The judge imposed a sentence of one year and one day in jail, but suspended it and then imposed a fine of $12,000. My body went limp with relief when I realized Euclide wasn't going to jail. Although he would be on probation for a while, his only real penalty would be the $12,000 fine. I looked at Euclide expecting to see a grateful person relieved by the fact he was not going to be incarcerated. But being the true cattle trader he was, without a second's hesitation Euclide turned to me and in a loud whisper said, "Ask the judge if he will take it at $1,000 per month." I turned to the judge and said, "Excuse me Your Honor," and then I turned back to Euclide, and grabbing his lapels, I said, "You're going to pay this right away!" I then turned back to the judge and said, "May we have thirty days, please, to pay the fine?" The judge, who I believe had overheard the entire exchange between Euclide and me, simply smiled and said, "That will be satisfactory, Mr. Langrock. The court is now in recess."

4. The Courthouse and Miscellaneous Characters

Two doors south of the courthouse on Court Street there is a large Victorian building. In the back of the building is a one bedroom apartment where my wife and I lived during the winter of 1960-1961. At the time, Hale's Funeral Parlor was located in the building between the courthouse and this residence. Its embalming room also served as a makeshift laboratory for use in forensic autopsies. Richard Woodruff was the state pathologist—an exceptionally bright man, a member of the so-called Harvard School of forensic science (Erie Stanley Gardner dedicated many of his Perry Mason mystery books to individual forensic pathologists from his group). Richard Woodruff had the kind of tenacious inquiring mind, coupled with a dry sense of humor, that makes for a perfect forensic pathologist.

AN ASIDE

On one occasion, Woodruff spoke at a Lions Club meeting and came armed with slides of the skeletal remains of three bodies that had been found in a shallow grave near the airport in East Middlebury. He explained how he could prove, from the type of damage done to their skulls, that these individuals had been murdered. He could also draw inferences concerning certain characteristics that could be attributed to the person who had committed the homicide. Unfortunately, no one was ever able to identify the remains. To this day the skeletons, which are now more than fifty years old, are still part of an unsolved mystery.

An untimely death—whether a homicide, suicide, accident, or just of unknown origin—had to be reported to the state's attorney, and the body could not be moved until the state's attorney had given the okay. I would try to be present whenever Dick Woodruff was doing an autopsy in Addison County. It could be argued that this was part of my duty as state's attorney, but in reality I was there out of curiosity. Dick was a wonderful teacher. I learned more about human anatomy and disease processes from watching him than from all other sources to which I have ever been exposed.

One day in 1963, a man died without explanation and, while there did not appear to be any possibility of foul play, I ordered an autopsy. The investigating officer was State Trooper Cleon McNally. Cleon was relatively new on the force. He had moved to Middlebury from Hardwick where he had been a car salesman before joining the state police. Later Cleon grew to like Middlebury better than his job with the state police, and he became a claims adjuster for the Middlebury Co-Operative Fire Insurance Company. Cleon was a typical Vermonter: soft-spoken, taciturn, and with the driest sense of humor. As he was the investigating officer, Cleon was requested to attend this particular autopsy. He was somewhat reluctant, as he was a bit squeamish, despite his imposing appearance as a state police officer.

The autopsy proceeded according to the usual protocol. First there was an examination of the outside of the body. Measurements were taken and observations were noted. The weight of the deceased was estimated, and unusual markings (tattoos, birthmarks, abrasions, signs of trauma, etc.) were recorded. After this process was completed, the internal organs were examined. An incision was made in the front of the body, opening up the entire chest and abdomen. The ribs were separated at the sternum and an examination was made of all the internal organs—the heart, liver, intestines, and so on—looking for signs as to the cause of death.

Cleon had managed quite well through the first part of the autopsy, but once the opening in the abdomen had been made and the examination of the organs started, he turned a pale green. Stoic as he was, he said nothing, and maintained his composure. Finally, the process of the internal examination completed, Dr. Woodruff went on to the next step—the examination of the brain. He took a sharp scalpel and cut the skin across the back of the neck from one ear to the other. He then peeled back the scalp, exposing the skull. He took an oscillating saw to the exposed skull, the saw vibrating back and forth in a manner which cut the bone without doing any damage to the soft tissue. It made a noise similar to that of a band saw cutting wood. Cleon, who had not said a single word since the beginning of the autopsy, finally turned to me and said, "Peter, if Doc keeps up that sawing, it's going to give that guy a headache."

On another occasion, Larry Hale, our neighboring funeral director, knocked on the door of our apartment about 6:30 at night. We were having some guests for a quiet dinner and a couple of beers. He asked if I could give him a hand. Our guest, Fred Neuberger, later the director of admissions at Middlebury College, agreed to help as well. Our task was to move a dead body from the hearse into the embalming room. The deceased was on a stretcher, and ordinarily Larry could have handled this himself, but this particular individual weighed something approaching 400 pounds. We helped Larry get the body into the building, and we then returned to our dinner. From time to time thereafter there were occasional remarks in town: "You never know what's going to happen when you have dinner at the Langrocks'."

AN ASIDE

The building in which our first apartment was located became the subject of potential litigation one weekend in the late 1970s. The owner of the building at that time decided that the structure was in need of a complete face-lift, and hired a local painter to undertake the job. One Saturday the painter put up his ladders and took down all of the shutters on the building in preparation for scraping and painting. The shutters were placed at the back of the property, near where the rubbish hauler picked up garbage and rubbish to be hauled off to the town dump. The rubbish hauler came to get the rubbish after the painter had quit for the day, and, seeing the old and somewhat misused shutters lying in the area where the rubbish was kept, took them off to the dump. The next day the owner arrived, saw that the shutters were missing, and talked to the painter, who was unaware that the shutters were gone. Together they figured out that the rubbish hauler must have carried them off. On reaching the rubbish hauler, they confirmed that the shutters had been taken to the dump; upon inquiry at the dump, it was discovered that they were already crushed and buried.

The building owner was sufficiently upset that the next day—even though it was Sunday—he called one of my partners, Mark Sperry, to ask who was legally responsible for the loss of the shutters. Mark told him that quite clearly it was the responsibility of the painter who had taken the shutters off and put them out back by the rubbish. Unknown to anybody else, on this very same Sunday the painter called another one of my partners, Jon Stahl, and asked him who was legally responsible for the loss of the shutters. Jon told him unequivocally that it was the rubbish hauler's fault for having hauled away the shutters to the dump. On this same day, still without knowledge of the other telephone calls, the rubbish hauler called my other partner, Fred Parker, to determine whose legal responsibility it was for the loss of the shutters. Parker told the rubbish hauler that it was obviously the owner's responsibility for allowing the painter to have put them where they were found and thought to be trash.

Our firm has the tradition of all the lawyers lunching together every day, unless they are tied up with a particular client or in court. On the Monday following the weekend of the shutters escapade, I was at lunch with Jon, Fred, and Mark. After exchanging a few pleasantries, Mark indicated that he had had a strange call over the weekend. He related that he had advised the owner of the house just two doors down from the courthouse that a painter who had taken the shutters off of the house and let them be carried away by the trash hauler was responsible for the loss of the shutters. At this point Jon Stahl said, "Oh no, you couldn't have said that, because I advised the painter that it was the trash hauler's responsibility." Fred quickly jumped in with, "You aren't going to believe this, but I advised the trash hauler that it was the owner's responsibility." In the course of a single weekend, we had given different advice to three different potential clients, each implicating one of our other potential clients as being liable for the occurrence.

Mark had enough presence of mind to inquire whether there was any insurance anywhere that would cover it. Fortunately, the homeowner's insurance did take care of it, and payment was made by the company for the loss of the shutters. We were off a rather embarrassing hook. (We later joked as to whom we should bill for the advice we had given. It was unanimously decided that this would be a true freebie.)

In the mid-1980s, Judge Edward Costello was the chief administrative judge for the state. He decided it was time to leave his fiefdom of Chittenden County, the next county north of Addison County, where he felt as if he knew the genealogy of every defendant who came before him. His first venture was to the City of Barre, in Washington County. The Washington County Bar held a banquet in his honor as he completed his six-month stint. At the conclusion of the banquet, Judge Costello was presented with a big box wrapped in fancy paper and tied up in ribbons. Inside the box was a confectionery—a cream puff. So much for the tough-guy image he liked to project. The next week he came to Addison County, where he was affectionately known as Judge Edward The Only.

Not all of the stuff law is made of actually occurs in the courtroom. Sometimes it happens in chambers.

A Middlebury woman was being prosecuted for disorderly conduct. Apparently, she had been ranting and raving at some children in the neighborhood, claiming they were picking on her and calling her "old wooden tit" because she had had a mastectomy. Whatever the appropriateness of the accusations may have been, they did not justify in the mind of the state her conduct in chasing after the children. The matter proceeded to trial with John Quinn prosecuting. The important character in this incident is Carol Craven, who as the court reporter, a position that holds more power in the governing of the court than would usually be believed—except by experienced trial lawyers. Carol went back into chambers with Judge Costello and said, "I am going to refuse to mark the exhibit." Judge Costello: "What exhibit are you talking about?" Carol: "The wooden tit, of course."

Judge Costello called the prosecutor and defense counsels into his chambers and asked Quinn, "Do you have some physical exhibits you wish to have admitted in this case?" Quinn wasn't quite sure what he was talking about, but he hemmed and hawed and indicated he couldn't think of any. The judge continued, "You're not going to try to have admitted any exhibit directly pertaining to a piece of anatomy?" Quinn looked even more puzzled and said, "No, I don't presently intend to introduce any such thing." The judge then explained that he thought he had a crisis on his hands because the court reporter was refusing to mark a particular exhibit. He then turned to Ms. Craven and smiled. "I think the problem is settled. The wooden tit will not be offered into evidence."

Jury drawings often bring out people's sense of humor—sometimes by the lawyer, sometimes by the judge, and sometimes by the potential juror. Occasionally, they have the effect of cutting down lawyers and litigants to an appropriate size. One of those occasions took place in the early 1970s. Ward Bedford, a state senator from Addison County for the previous ten years, was a party in some litigation before the superior court. As a senior senator, Ward considered himself closer to God than to the other members of the senate, and he was thought to be autocratic and egotistical. At the jury draw, Ward's attorney looked towards the eighteen persons taken from the panel for possible selection as the final jurors. Fully expecting wide recognition of their state senator, his client, he asked how many of them knew personally or had heard of Ward Bedford. Much to the chagrin of Ward Bedford and his counsel, no one raised a hand, and the smiles on the faces of his opposition gave joy to Mudville that day.

Another jury-drawing story goes back to when I was a young state's attorney. It was my first trial opposing Jack Conley. Jack was aware that I had matriculated through the New York City public school system, and had only spent summers in Vermont, except for part of one year when I was in school in Middlebury. I went to college and law school at the University of Chicago and then returned to Middlebury to run for state's attorney. In this particular case, Jack

Conley was going to make sure the jurors knew I was an outsider, a flatlander, and not a Vermont native.

This attack was a bit hypocritical from Jack, who had been raised in Brockton, Massachusetts, and had come to Middlebury College on a baseball athletic scholarship. He lettered in three sports but his greatest love was always baseball. Jack ended up staying in Middlebury for the rest of his life.

On this occasion Jack looked at the jury and said, "Do any of you know Mr. Langrock?" There were three hands that went up. One was that of a sweet-looking elderly lady in the front row of the jury. Jack looked at her, approached her with his best courtroom swagger, and, in an attempt to accent my newcomer status, asked, "And how long have you known him?" She looked at Jack and said, "Well, since he was about that high," holding her hand about three feet off the ground. "I used to tie his shoes in the morning." As a toddler, I used to get up early to watch her husband making dough-nuts as the baker at the Lake Dunmore Hotel. He would always manage to fry up a few doughnut holes just for me, and his wife, the juror, would tie my shoe laces. Jack abandoned that line of inquiry.

Defendants coming into the Addison County Courthouse for arraignment were sometimes met with unusual circumstances. One of the most unusual was when Bill Mikell was sitting in Addison County as the district court judge. Bill had a back problem and for a while he could not sit on the bench in the courtroom. The only way he could get relief was to lie flat on his back. Instead of going into the courtroom and then being called to the bar to enter their pleas, defendants were ushered into the hallway outside of Bill's chambers, which were on the first floor in the southeast corner of the courthouse. One at a time the defendants were brought into chambers with their counsel, and Bill would take their plea while lying flat on his back on the floor. Somehow this did not coincide with the defendants' usual image of what an arraignment should be, and it certainly was unlike anything they had ever seen on television.

On one occasion, my then-partner Fred Parker arrived with his client. (Fred now sits as the fourth Vermonter ever on the United States Court of Appeals for the Second Circuit.) His client was a ruddy-faced Irishman who had been charged with driving while under the influence. His alcohol test had been high, and Fred had decided to plead him guilty as soon as possible, hoping for only a fine and the usual license suspension. Neither Fred nor his client had yet been exposed to the unusual position the judge would be in when their turn came to go into chambers. They walked into the room, and a state of shock appeared on both Fred's face and that of his client. Fred recovered quickly and said, "Your Honor, what happened?" The judge, lying flat on the floor, staring straight up to the ceiling, said, "I got hit by a drunk driver last weekend." The complexion on the client's face went from ruddy to a pale gray instantly and never recovered its color, even when the judge added, "Only kidding."

5. Dr. Woodard & Porter Hospital

In 1960, the medical profession in Middlebury looked substantially different from what it does today. There were seven doctors: one a general surgeon, one an internist, and the rest were family practitioners. Porter Hospital was one small building, located on the outskirts of the town of Middlebury, looking out over adjoining dairy farms and Otter Creek. The hospital was run by a board of trustees consisting of locally prominent persons who had little specialized knowledge about running a hospital. The charter of the hospital, which had been incorporated in 1941, was amended in 1952 to give every resident of Addison County and the town of Brandon, over the age of twenty-one, a vote as a member of the corporation.

In 1962, one of the local doctors was Richard Woodard. Dr. Woodard had had a sound medical education and a stint in the public health service working with Indian tribes, after which he had come to Middlebury to open his family practice. He did not fit the typical mold of a Vermont doctor, which was white, male, Christian, and Republican. Dick Woodard was a Democrat, a Jew, and a believer in a strong national health-care policy that would provide adequate medical care for the poor and disadvantaged. His personal goals were focused on his patients and their health rather than on his pocketbook.

In 1962, Porter Hospital had three levels of surgical privileges. The highest, or "A" privileges, gave the doctor permission to do every type of surgery. The only doctor qualifying for this category was the general surgeon, Ray Collins. Ray was an old-time Vermonter, a very careful surgeon, who sometimes believed the hospital was his personal domain. He also had a second love, a registered Holstein dairy herd at his home farm in Colchester, Vermont.

The second surgical category was a limited one, or "B" privileges. This allowed the general practitioners, and family practitioners, to perform a large number of medical services they were clearly capable of doing. There was also a third category, or the "C" privileges, which allowed the physicians little more than the use of Band-Aids. Except for Ray Collins, all of the Middlebury physicians had Class "B" privileges.

In the hospital regulations defining what was permitted in Class "B" and Class "A" surgeries, there was some confusion in connection with the treatment of patients who had received serious burns. The general medical nomenclature concerning first-, second-, and third-degree burns had been changed, but the hospital's definitions had not.

On one occasion a young girl, about nine years old, had been severely burned. She was a patient of Dr. Woodard's and he arrived at the hospital, saw her in the emergency room, tended to her admission, and carefully treated her. He did so with sufficient caring and skill that not only did the patient recover, but the *Addison County Independent* ran a front-page article extolling Dr. Woodard's skill and care, which had resulted in this wonderful outcome. This article apparently stuck in the craw of members of the medical staff who made a complaint that the young girl's burn was sufficiently severe to have been treated only by someone with "A" hospital privileges. They charged that Dr. Woodard had only "B" privileges and that his treatment of the patient was not respectful of the hospital rules. Accordingly, Woodard should have turned the case over to Collins and not continued treating the patient himself. The fact of a positive outcome for the child was apparently insignificant as compared to the maintenance of hospital discipline.

The medical staff heard arguments about the confusion and responsibilities over which burns fell into the "A" category and which fell into the "B" category. They concluded that Dr. Woodard had violated hospital policy. As a result of this transgression, the medical staff thought it necessary to discipline Dr. Woodard, and did so by putting him on probation for one year and reducing his surgical privileges to Class "C," although all agreed he was qualified to perform services in the Class "B" category. This position of the medical staff was ratified by the board of trustees.

During the course of the following year, another patient of Dr. Woodard's, also a young child, presented an injured arm which had been fractured. The fracture was rather straightforward, and it was certainly within Dr. Woodard's abilities to treat it. He did so successfully. Once again, however, he was called before the board because this procedure was claimed to have fallen into the Class "B" category, and as he was on probation for one year and limited to the Class "C" category, he had again transgressed the hospital's rules. The fact that the treatment was successful, and the fact that it was in the patient's interest from a convenience standpoint to have Dr. Woodard treat it, were bypassed, and the medical staff disciplined Dr. Woodard by voting to expel him from the hospital and terminating his surgical privileges. Again, the board of nine trustees unanimously adopted the medical staff's recommendation.

When these actions became generally known in the community, a segment of the public became seriously upset. Dr. Woodard's patients were loyal, not only because of the quality service he performed, but also because of his genuine concern about their health, and because of his practice of treating large and poor families at substantially reduced rates or completely free. This group prepared for the annual meeting of the members of the corporation. The meeting usually was an event where the trustees and a few friends got together to elect the slate of trustees for the next year. On this particular occasion, several hundred people showed up, and an opposition slate of three trustees who were favorably inclined toward Dr. Woodard were nominated from the floor and elected. As the trustees served a three-year staggered term, six of those who had acted to revoke Dr. Woodard's privileges were still on the board. The meeting had been held at the elementary-school gymnasium to an over-flowing crowd. It received front-page coverage in the *Addison County Independent* and the entire subject became the conversation from barber shops to cocktail parties. Efforts to have Dr. Woodard reinstated during the year came to no avail. The trustees continued their position by the now 6-3 vote. As the year wore on, the entire community was bracing for the next annual meeting where it would be determined whether Dr. Woodard's supporters could elect three additional trustees who would tip the scales in his favor.

The six holdover trustees expressed concern that they did not have any effective way to determine exactly who were the twenty-one-year-old residents of Addison County and the town of Brandon—thus members of the corporation and eligible to vote—at the upcoming meeting. They called a special meeting to amend the charter to add an additional qualification for membership in the form of a minimal annual contribution to the hospital of one dollar. The holdover trustees thought this was a logical way to control access to the ballot box, while the Woodard supporters thought this was a method of controlling access to the ballot box by excluding those who for one reason or another had not made the contribution in advance. It was clearly intended as a step to prevent the Woodard forces from stacking the meeting and electing their choice of trustees. Drives were started by both sides to get people to make the one-dollar contribution and get on the voting list for the annual meeting.

Formal notice for the annual meeting was placed in the newspapers, as required in the bylaws. Less formal notice—by way of newspaper articles, the one dollar donation drive, and word-of-mouth—ensured a large participation. Recognizing that this had become a matter of substantial controversy, the trustees decided to hold the meeting in the Middlebury College Field House, which was the only facility of sufficient size to accommodate the anticipated turnout. More than 1,700 people came to the meeting. This is truly an extra-ordinary number when you realize that the total population for the Porter Hospital's immediate geographic area was no more than 20,000.

At the meeting, the Woodard supporters challenged the trustees of the corporation for acting to change the bylaws. A charge of dis-enfranchisement was made which claimed that the contract right (which was felt to be akin to a stockholder's right) had in effect been extinguished when a monetary figure was adopted as a threshold to participation in the hospital corporation. If a one-dollar contribution was acceptable, could a one-hundred-dollar contribution or even a one-thousand-dollar contribution be required?

The other side took issue with this position and claimed that what was being accomplished was simply a reasonable way to have people focus on the activities of the hospital, and to allow certain controls over what amounted to a voter registration list. Myron Samuelson of Burlington, counsel for the hospital, was present. Before this large audience, he played the role of elder statesman, and belittled the disenfranchisement position. Having originally put forward that position, I felt the belittling was directed at me personally. I decided I would take Samuelson to court on it if the Woodard forces lost. This they did, as they were not able to muster a majority from the 1,700 persons present, and the trustees who had supported the revocation of privileges were re-elected.

The next day saw the first of three trips made from the Addison County Courthouse to the Vermont Supreme Court dealing with this controversy. A petition in chancery styled *Langrock v. Porter Hospital, Inc.* was filed, claiming that the act of the hospital in requiring the one-dollar contribution was an act of disenfranchisement and violated the contract provisions of both the United States Constitution and the Constitution of Vermont. The hospital made a motion to dismiss my claim and Judge Dale Brooks, acting as chancellor, granted the motion. I filed an appeal with the Vermont Supreme Court, and on February 7, 1967, the supreme court affirmed Judge Brooks' action in dismissing my petition,[3] saying that the contract rights of the individuals who had been members of the corporation included the statutory provisions for amending the membership requirements, and if the amendment had been done according to statute, the provision of one dollar was reasonable. Therefore, although the action was deemed a disenfranchisement, it was permissible.

Prior to this meeting, Dr. Woodard had been to see me. He asked if the courts could afford him any direct relief and get him readmitted as a member of the staff. We discussed the facts of the situation and we found that Porter Hospital had received funds from the federal government under the Hill-Burton Act. It had received funds from the state of Vermont and from local municipalities as well. If Porter Hospital were a public hospital, with public funding, Dr. Woodard might be entitled to certain due-process rights by way of notice and a hearing prior to his dismissal. We decided to bring a petition in chancery calling for his reinstatement. It was duly filed in the court, charging that the hospital and the medical staff (which was also named as a defendant) had improperly excluded Dr. Woodard from the hospital. The defendant filed a motion to dismiss the case, saying that even if the facts were true, the courts could give no relief because it was a private hospital and they had complete control over their own internal affairs. A hearing on that motion was held before Natt Divoll, sitting as a chancellor. Surprisingly, rather than simply deciding the motion as a matter of law, he took some evidence. After hearing the evidence, he denied the motion by the hospital and the medical staff to dismiss, and ordered that Dr. Woodard be given the reasons for his dismissal as well as a hearing to determine in fact whether the reasons were valid. This hearing in the first instance would be before the board of trustees of the hospital itself, but if the board acted arbitrarily, there was the possibility of a further hearing before the court.

The hospital was quite upset about this result, as it was the first time they would have to specify publicly the charges about Dr. Woodard allegedly violating the hospital's regulations dealing with surgical categories. It was also the first opportunity for Dr. Woodard to face his accusers. The hospital immediately filed an appeal to the Vermont Supreme Court. Briefs were duly submitted and we took a trip to Montpelier. Both the hospital and Dr. Woodard were anxious to have the court deal with the substantive issues raised by the motion to dismiss. However, in an opinion by Justice Shangraw, the court decided on its own motion that it had no jurisdiction because the denial by that trial court of the motion to dismiss was not a final judgment and, therefore, the only thing that would have been appropriate was an interlocutory appeal[4]—one that is taken before a matter is finally decided. However, such an appeal requires permission of the supreme court, which had not been granted in the case.

With the appeal dismissed, we went back before the Addison Superior Court. This time, the hospital got its ducks in a row and applied to the chancellor for permission to appeal on certain certified questions of law. The chancellor certified two questions: 1) Whether or not the Court of Chancery erred in denying the defendant's motion to dismiss; and 2) Whether or not the order dated December 9, 1964, was appropriate under the jurisdiction of the Court of Chancery, if such jurisdiction existed.

We were thus set for another argument before the Vermont

Supreme Court. Once again, briefs were duly filed. The hospital argued that it was a private hospital and the courts had no right to interfere with its management. On behalf of Dr. Woodard, I argued that there were sufficient funds from local, state, and federal sources to classify the hospital as a public hospital, one which had to comply with the due-process requirements. This all took place before the 1970s rebirth of civil rights suits. We found ourselves in a case before the Vermont Supreme Court which they considered to be one of "first impression," for which there were no existing legal precedents.

On the day of oral argument, I was reading the *Burlington Free Press* comic section. One of the strips was "Rex Morgan, M.D.," and it was one I seldom more than glanced at. On this particular day, however, the strip dealt with the importance of a hospital to a doctor and how without access to it the doctor was virtually barred from practice. I cut out that strip and took it to the supreme court with me. In the course of oral argument, I pulled out the strip from my file and said, "Your Honors, the practical effect of what has happened to Dr. Woodard is even recognized in the comic strips. Just this morning in 'Rex Morgan, M.D.,' they pointed out how important hospital privileges are to a doctor." It may be the only time a comic strip was directly cited to the Vermont Supreme Court for purposes of precedent. After a full hour of argument by the two sides, the court took the matter under advisement.

In 1965, the supreme court held five terms of court a year. This case was argued at the December term, and the decision was handed down on the opening day of the February term. The five justices filed out of chambers and up onto their elevated seats behind the bench at the head of the walnut-paneled courtroom. Chief Justice Holden announced that several decisions were being handed down that day, and he turned to Justice Shangraw who proceeded to read to the assemblage his opinion in *Woodard v. Porter Hospital, Inc. and Medical Staff of Porter Hospital, Inc.*[5] It was the custom at that time for a member of the court to read aloud from the bench the entire opinion in certain cases the court felt were particular significant. This tradition has been lost, unfortunately, and now the decisions are simply filed with the clerk's office and made available to the press and the Internet.

As I was sitting there listening to the opinion being read, Justice Shangraw started demolishing my arguments one after the other. First, he demolished the concept that Porter Hospital was anything other than a private hospital. He went through its corporate structure and then into the funds it received, and came to the conclusion that indeed Porter Hospital was a private hospital and not a public institution. My heart sank lower. He then went on to explain the broad latitude given to private institutions in dealing with their business affairs. I figured it was all over. Suddenly the opinion took a twist. Justice Shangraw, continuing, indicated that even private institutions, when charged with a public interest, had certain fiduciary responsibilities. The hospital could not act arbitrarily and capriciously in detriment to that public interest. The decision went on to affirm the chancellor's holding denying the motion to dismiss, and sent the case back to the Addison County Chancery Court for further hearing to determine if the acts of the hospital in dismissing Dr. Woodard from the medical staff had indeed been arbitrary or capricious. The case was a breakthrough precedent in giving the courts some oversight over the activities of private charitable corporations.

If this was an important case to me as a young lawyer; it was even more important to my client as a physician, for both his reputation and his ability to practice medicine were at stake. The roller-coaster ride of listening to Justice Shangraw reading his opinion, which moved from the impression of a loss to the joys of victory all in a matter of a few minutes, is something one does not easily forget.

Unfortunately, this story has a tragic end. While we were preparing for the trial on the merits of our case, Dr. Woodard, suffering under the stress, had a nervous breakdown, and was institutionalized. On the third anniversary of his dismissal from the hospital, he committed suicide.

6. Bucky Dragon and the Great Scallop Caper

Hanford Davis—"Hamp" as he was known to his friends—was a marvelously gifted trial lawyer. His low-key approach to matters, his sense of humor, and his tough, hardhitting cross-examination made him one of the really competent trial lawyers in Vermont. I first met Hamp in the summer of 1958. He was working with Wynn Underwood on a petition to modify a trust that was being heard in the Addison County Court. The Addison County Agricultural Society was the owner of the fairgrounds located east of Court Street and south of the courthouse. There had been no agricultural fair held there since before World War II and the purpose of the court action was to allow for a change of the use of the lands from agricultural fairgrounds to permit them to be conveyed to the town of Middlebury to be used to build a new elementary school. The court granted the petition and the land is now occupied by the Mary Hogan School and the town recreational facilities.

In the summer of 1959, Ted Murin, the state's attorney, was ill, and Bill Burrage was appointed special assistant attorney general for the purpose of prosecuting a burglary that had occurred at the Chevrolet dealership, which was then Beckwith Motors and is now Shea Motors. Three people were charged with the crime: a twenty-two-year-old, a sixteen-year-old, and a fifteen-year-old. The sixteen-year-old was Robert "Bucky" Dragon. Hanford Davis defended Bucky. Judge Harold "Hack" Sylvester was the presiding judge.

Bill Burrage asked me if I could take leave of my clerkship duties with Wynn Underwood for a week or so and assist him as a law clerk in the trial of the case, and of course I was delighted to do so. It was a circumstantial case, and the key pieces of evidence were a footprint that matched Bucky's boots, found outside the automobile showroom, and particles of safe insulation taken from his clothes. Analyzed by the FBI labs, the particles proved to have come from the Beckwith Motors safe, which had been partially broken open during the burglary. The prosecutor had to prove the chain of evidence from the police to the laboratory and then back to court, and prove the integrity of that chain. It was the first time FBI agents came to the Addison County Courthouse from their laboratories to give evidence in the form of scientific opinion.

The case went on quite smoothly, and despite the testimony of Virginia Dragon, Bucky's mother, that he was home in bed at the time the burglary took place, the jury reached a verdict of guilty. Hack Sylvester had instructed the jury in a heavy-handed way, not only in words but with vocal emphasis and facial expression. A bit disgusted by this, and while the judge was still instructing the jury, Hamp passed a note to Bill. It read, "Why doesn't he just direct a verdict and be done with it?"

In those days, pre-sentence investigations, which help put a defendant and the crime in context, were not required. In Bucky Dragon's case, the jury's verdict was rendered at about two o'clock, and the court immediately proceeded to sentencing. By three-thirty that afternoon, sixteen-year-old Bucky Dragon had been convicted of his first offense of burglary, and he was on his way to Windsor State Prison to do a three-to-five-year term.

In subsequent proceedings, the fifteen-year-old was treated as a juvenile and found to be a delinquent. He was sent to the Weeks School in Vergennes. (The Weeks School is now operated by the Job Corps, but at that time it was a residential campus for approximately 250 juveniles and run more like a boarding school than a reform school. The youngsters attended Vergennes High School, and were well treated. Many went on to college and made true successes of their lives.)

The third man, at twenty-two the only adult involved in the burglary, was represented by Jack Conley. Ted Murin recovered his health and resumed his duties as state's attorney. Murin was finally convinced by Conley to enter into a plea agreement whereby Conley's client entered a plea of guilty to petty larceny and paid a one-hundred-dollar fine. The grossly disproportionate punishments for those acting in the same offense put a chip on Bucky's shoulder that lasted him the rest of his life.

Bucky became a bit of a folk hero and was constantly in and out of trouble. He was well over six feet tall, solidly built, and ruggedly handsome. Every time he went into a bar, somebody would always be there who thought of him as the "King of the Mountain" and wanted to try to knock him off his hill. Sometimes he couldn't resist responding, and the initiator of the conflict was always sorry he started it. Bucky was from Ripton, summer home of the poet, Robert Frost. Ripton was also a favorite haunt of the game wardens, and, in a mountain-town tradition, Bucky enjoyed testing them. Not all the venison he ever ate was taken during open season.

Sometime in the early 1970s came the "Great Scallop Caper," in which Bucky was involved, though only in a peripheral way. Someone highjacked a truck full of scallops down in Rhode Island. The truck made its way to Vermont, where the scallops were peddled at a very attractive price to dozens of restaurants between Rutland and Burlington. The people orchestrating the peddling of the scallops were from Brandon. They claimed the scallops were obtained as a result of a labor dispute on the coast. At some point the young men actually peddling the truckload of scallops got suspicious themselves as to its origins. After the full load had been sold, there came the question as to what to do with the truck. Bucky, who was an operator par excellence of heavy machinery, used a large bulldozer to dig a hole in a field in another mountain town just south of Ripton, Goshen. The hole he bulldozed was big enough so that the truck could be driven into it and buried.

The persons who participated in the sale of the scallops were eventually brought to justice through the U.S. Attorney's Office, and the time came to unbury the truck as evidence. What everyone had forgotten was that in the truck when it was buried were a couple of barrels of lobster bait. This lobster bait had ripened to an unbelievable degree of olfactory potency. When the truck was uncovered and the doors opened, the searchers ran for cover and the stench fouled the air for miles around.

Despite his continued rebellion against authority, Bucky was a person whose word was good. When he was not drinking, he could be thoroughly trusted. He never lacked for work, and was one of the Poma Ski Lift Company's best employees. When Bucky was killed in an accident where a log skidder rolled over on him in March of 1980, the funeral in Brandon was the largest in anyone's memory. The church was full and hundreds of people waited outside to pay their respects.

In a different era, instead of being known as an outlaw, Bucky might well have been regarded as a real hero, as he had the intelligence, strength, and energies to be one. Many people think he was and still is.

7. Drunk Driving

Over the years, much of the district court activity in the Addison County Courthouse has involved drunk driving cases. More cases of drunk driving go to trial than any other criminal charge. The reason for this is that a conviction of the charge brings with it suspension of a driver's license for a substantial length of time. In a rural community like Addison County, where there is no public transportation system, the loss of a driver's license completely destroys mobility. This often means that on top of the criminal penalties, the defendant will also lose his or her job.

In 1960 the public had a much greater tolerance for the offense than they do now. It wasn't until 1958 that the legislature first passed the so-called implied consent law, where a suspected drunk driver was given the option of either submitting to a chemical test or automatically losing his or her license. The original permissible limit was.15 percent of alcohol in the blood stream. The defendant was given the choice of a breath test, a blood test, or a urine test. The urine test was the most unreliable measure of alcohol content in the bloodstream, especially for women: at that time all the police officers in Addison County were men, and when a woman was arrested for DWI she was afforded privacy to produce a urine sample. You could almost count on the fact that the sample would be diluted by water from either the toilet itself or from the faucet at the wash basin.

The breath test also had a margin of error, although arguably a smaller one. The only accurate measure was the blood test, and few defendants opted for that. In practice a person had to have a reading of substantially more than.15 percent in order to convince a jury that a conviction was appropriate. The cultural norms at that time basically permitted drinking and driving, unless you were really pretty drunk. To put it in perspective, at one point the state pathologist, Dick Woodruff, testified that it was impossible to drink enough beer to get your test over.15 percent.

On one occasion in the early 1960s a defendant did opt for a blood test, and, pursuant to law, this test had to be administered by a doctor. Dr. Woodard was called to the county jail to take the man's blood. The test came back at about.20 percent, and he was duly charged with DWI. The defendant hired Gerry Trudeau as his defense counsel. A jury was empaneled, and the trial began.

As a first witness, the state called Dr. Woodard to testify that he had gone to the jail, drawn blood, and had properly preserved it for shipment to the laboratory. On cross-examination, Trudeau asked the doctor whether he took precautions when he drew blood from a prisoner to make sure there would be no infection from the blood-letting process. The doctor said he certainly did. To Trudeau's next inquiry, "How do you do that"," he said, "I carefully swab the area with alcohol before I put the needle in." The possibility of the needle used to draw the blood being contaminated by the doctor's alcohol was slight, but enough to make me recognize that the state was better off accepting a plea of guilty to a reduced charge rather than going to verdict on the DWI.

In the first DWI case I prosecuted to trial, the defendant was a fellow by the name of Murray. Murray was defended by Jack Conley and the laboratory evidence showed a.24 percent test. A state police officer had noticed Murray's erratic driving and saw him pull into his driveway. He pursued Murray into the driveway where he found him and a drinking buddy standing next to the car. Both of them were obviously quite impaired. After I had presented the state's case, the court decided that the evidence was sufficient to deny the defendant's motion for an acquittal, indicating that the state had put in sufficient evidence to sustain a conviction. It was uncertain as to what defense Jack was going to put forward. He called his client to the stand.

Murray related where he had been that night and how much he actually had had to drink. He testified that he had started at noon, when he had three beers; on to the afternoon, when he had finished a six-pack; to before dinner, when he consumed another six-pack. After dinner, during the course of the same evening, he went to a bar where he admitted to drinking another seven or eight beers. He topped it off with one or two beers on his way home. Jack Conley then asked the question, "Do you consider yourself as being drunk that evening?" The witnessed answered, "I certainly do." This was followed up with the next question, "Then why were you driving?" The defendant answered, "I wasn't driving. I was too drunk to drive. It was my buddy who was driving the car." On rebuttal the state police officer testified that he distinctly saw Mr. Murray driving the car before pulling into his driveway, and the jury did convict.

Salisbury is a town just south of Middlebury, and, during my tenure as state's attorney, one of Salisbury's leading citizens was Harry Sullivan. Harry had a truly fine mind and an erudite way of speaking. He also loved to drink. It was often quoted in Salisbury that Harry knew more dead drunk than the rest of the men in town put together did sober.

One evening there was an accident on the new stretch of Route 7 leading from Salisbury past the old Howard Foster farm towards the Poor Farm Bridge. A tractor-trailer had collided with a manure spreader being driven by a local farmer, René Cloutier. René was a farmer of French-Canadian background, and he not only sounded the part, he looked the part. He wasn't more than 5'4" tall, but he was as tough as they come. The state police had been called to the scene, and two cruisers were there with their red lights flashing. (In the 1960s the state police cars were still equipped with red, not blue, lights.) The police had also put out several flares to warn motorists proceeding north on Route 7 of the presence of the fifteen-foot-long wagon-like manure spreader in the traveled lane.

Harry, who had imbibed more than a little that evening, drove right past the flares and into the manure spreader without even slowing down. The manure spreader was heaved into the air and it landed squarely on top of René Cloutier, who had been standing next to it. The police quickly rushed over to see if René was okay. René climbed out from under the spreader, shook himself, and said, "What in hell happened?" Recognizing that by some miracle René wasn't seriously hurt, State Trooper Rodney Mott went over to the vehicle that had hit the spreader. Behind the wheel he found Harry Sullivan. Rodney looked at Harry who was well known to him and said, "Harry, what the hell are you doing? Didn't you see all those lights? You didn't even slow down." Harry, without missing a beat, said, "I saw so many lights, I thought somebody had opened up a new hot dog stand." Harry was prosecuted for DWI but was never convicted, as he had cancer and died before the case came to trial.

In 1961, Alan Stone was arrested on a DWI charge. Joe Wool was retained by Stone and decided to test the mettle of the new state's attorney. It was a close case, and Joe had done his usual good job challenging the state's evidence, which he completed just before the noon recess. Joe's work, however, went for naught, for when the court reconvened at 1:30 p.m., the defendant was sitting in his chair with a flushed face, a bright red nose, and the unmistakable aroma of alcohol surrounding him. Joe could not possibly put his client on the stand, and, while appearing drunk in court during a drunk-driving trial is not conclusive as to whether the defendant was drunk on the night of the offense, the jury did not take much time to convict him.

AN ASIDE

The court reporter on the *Stone* case was Marguerite Stebbins. Maggie was fresh out of Vergennes Union High School, where she had been the outstanding secretarial student. This was her first stint at court reporting. After the conviction was obtained, Maggie and I and the two state police officers involved went down Merchants Row to Lockwood's Restaurant, where we all had a beer. On the way back from

court, the officers asked Maggie about her career, and Rodney
Mott asked her how old she was. She said, "Nineteen," at
which point everybody gulped, realizing we had just participated in obtaining beer for a minor.

Shortly after the *Stone* case, Maggie Stebbins, who had been the
court reporter in that case, went to work in Burlington as Joe Wool's
secretary. Joe had filed an appeal of the *Stone* case to the Vermont
Supreme Court. He actually had no grounds for an appeal, but he
was instructed by his client to take one anyway. In the appeal papers,
Joe claimed he had taken a general exception to the charge given by
the judge to the jury. An exception is usually made at the bench after
the judge has charged the jury; the lawyer points out that the judge
possibly made errors of law in instructing the jury. The transcript did
not reflect that Joe had taken any exceptions whatsoever. He then
claimed the record was incomplete as it was taken by a court
reporter in her first case and that she had failed to record a general
exception he had made after the Judge's charge. Maggie was now
working for him and when she found out she was to be blamed in
the supreme court papers for having failed to record properly what
had been going on in the lower court, it did not sit well with her. It
does not sit well with her to this day. She let Joe know how she felt
about it at the time, and even today (she is now the chief court
reporter in the state court system) she still chides him on it.

In due time the Vermont Supreme Court ruled that there was
no record of Joe taking a general exception and even if Joe had
taken a "general exception," there was no such thing recognized in
Vermont, as all exceptions had to specifically draw the court's attention to those portions of the Judge's charge to which the defendant
was excepting. The court then went on to say that besides, there was
nothing in the charge that could be excepted to. It's the only
Vermont Supreme Court case where a lawyer lost on three separate
grounds: (1) that there was no general exception made; (2) that
there is no such thing as a general exception; and (3) even if there
were, there was nothing to except to.[6]

8. Some Individuals of the 1960s

In 1960, the Addison County courthouse housed the superior court, which also included most of the activities of what is now family court; the municipal court, which handled most of the criminal and juvenile cases; and the probate court. It also housed the private law offices of Charles O. Adams. After my election as state's attorney in November of 1960, I approached the side judges to see if they could make some office space available to me. They gave me the back two rooms in the northeast corner of the building. Many of the trials and tribulations of building a law practice from scratch occurred in those offices. The job of state's attorney was part-time. It took up about one-half of my time, and I was able to spend the rest of it in private practice, using my offices in the courthouse for that purpose.

In the summer of 1961 my wife Joann was working as my secretary. A young man came in and asked to see me. My
secretary/wife asked him for his name. He said, "That is just the
problem I'm here to see Mr. Langrock about. My name is Hoar:
'H-O-A-R.'" He was a junior high school teacher whose students
were having too much fun calling him Mr. Hoar, and he wished to
change his name. We prepared the appropriate papers and walked
him down to the probate court where in due course his name was
changed to another family name that stirred less mirth in the minds
of his junior high school students.

In 1962, a man named John Bouchard came into my office on
the referral of my good friend Bill Rule. Mr. Bouchard inquired as
to the cost of setting up a Vermont corporation to operate as a
building construction company. I quoted him a fee of three hundred
dollars. He produced a roll of greenbacks and flashed several one-
hundred dollar bills. He pulled three from the pack and then said,
"Is it okay if I give you just one hundred dollars right now and pay
you the rest later?" Eager as I was for a new client, and impressed as
I was with the roll of cash, I took the one-hundred dollar retainer
and set up the corporation. I never got the other two hundred dollars. But that is only the beginning of the story.

Bouchard went into the business of building garages at bargain
basement prices. His company boomed, and he soon moved into
residential housing. He developed a connection with the Central
Vermont Public Service Corporation and became the largest builder
of electric-heated homes in the state. Bouchard's building company
was so active that he constantly needed more workers. Almost sin-
gle-handedly he raised the prevailing wage rate for carpenters from
$1.50 to $3.00 an hour. He built a store and a campground along-
side the New Haven River in the stretch leading from Bristol to
Lincoln. He also built a nice home in Lincoln where he, his wife,
two children, and a boxer dog lived. Bouchard drove a Lincoln
Continental with a car phone, which was then quite a novelty; he
certainly was my only client who had one.

Bouchard made all sorts of deals, borrowed all sorts of money,
and was becoming a well-known financier in the county. As his business grew, he was able to borrow substantial sums from the Bristol
National Bank based upon his signature alone, and the bank
appeared very happy to have his business. In contrast, most long-
time residents of Bristol could only borrow much smaller amounts,
and then only upon giving security that absolutely protected the

bank. In fact, the bank was generally viewed as rather parsimonious in granting loans to locals. Nonetheless, most people were glad to see the bank support the real economic growth that was caused by Bouchard's construction work and his financial dealings.

One day all this ended. Some neighbors complained that the Bouchard dog was tied up outside his home barking, and that the Bouchards had not been seen for two or three days. It was in the early fall of the year and John Bouchard had been nominated as the Democratic candidate for the state senate in the upcoming elections. Given his business know-how and the resulting stimulation of what had been a rather stagnant economic condition in the country, it was thought that he might win. This was despite the fact he was a Democrat in a heavily Republican area. Moreover, he avoided having his picture taken for press purposes. Now an investigation of the Bouchards' house revealed no trace of John Bouchard, his wife, or children—only a hungry dog.

About three weeks later the news trickled back that the Lincoln Continental with the car phone had been found in the parking area of the Cincinnati airport. This was the last anyone ever heard of John Bouchard and his family. It then came to light that before disappearing he had obtained $31,000 in cash as proceeds from an unsecured loan at the Bristol bank. The bank was going to have to eat the loss. Over the next several months, an investigation revealed that this was not the first time John Bouchard had gone into a community, stirred up some economic activity, taken the local bank for some money, and moved on—under a variety of aliases. Once he had posed as an army colonel in a western state, and another time he had perpetrated frauds in a similar fashion in Virginia, under the alias of Kelly. He was already on the FBI's wanted list for various frauds, and the authorities believed that he moved on to a new location because he caught wind they might be closing in.

Bankruptcy papers were filed by his creditors and the few remaining assets became part of the bankruptcy estate. Mark Sperry, now my partner, who was then practicing in Burlington, became trustee of the bankruptcy estate. An auction was held and I purchased two or three silver trophies that Bouchard had apparently won some years before in a skeet-shooting competition. I still have those pieces today, and occasionally for some party I bring them out and am reminded of John.

The amazing thing about John Bouchard was that he was an extremely intelligent, charming, forceful individual. On one occasion, Bill and Charmaine Rule, Joann and I, and John and his wife decided to journey to Green Mountain Park, a race track located in the town of Pownal in the southwestern part of Vermont, just north of the Massachusetts line. On the way down John insisted upon buying dinner. Not only did he insist upon buying dinner, he insisted upon choosing the menu, and everybody ate shrimp cocktails and steak.

John Bouchard was a competent sportsman, could handle a shotgun well, and appeared to enjoy hunting. He certainly was in fact a skilled builder. The man was a true enigma. No one has ever been able to figure out how he could leave a community with his wife and two children, take off, and set up someplace else under a different alias without ever being traced. In today's world of credit cards and computers this probably would not be as easy, or even possible at all. In any case, to my knowledge he has never been heard of as John Bouchard since.

The Bristol community was not totally upset by his passage through their community. He had gained a good reputation, stimulated the local economy and, best of all, many felt, had taken the Bristol bank for $31,000.00—the same bank that was so stingy about making loans to lifelong residents of the village.

Some months after he disappeared I was in Bristol doing a title search, and I took a break intending to have lunch at one of the local restaurants. I found myself without any money and went to the Bristol bank and asked for a counter check so that I could draw five dollars in cash on my account at the National Bank of Middlebury. The teller accommodated me and handed me a check and, while I was in the process of filling it out, one of the other persons in line said, "Peter, haven't you got one of Bouchard's checks?" The general mirth of the customers was not appreciated by the teller and the other bank employees.

A young lawyer trying to build a practice is always on the lookout for clients. I had established a working relationship with a fairly prominent and affluent farmer in Shoreham by the name of Nellie Fry. She came to see me often, with her brother in tow, to deal with a variety of relatively minor matters, and I had worked hard to develop a good rapport with her. Unfortunately, she died. Her brother was designated as the executor of her estate. One day at the courthouse I saw him coming up the hallway in the general direction of my office. I figured he was looking for me to possibly do work in connection with the Nellie Fry estate. He greeted me cordially and then walked past me into the office of Charlie Adams. I was a bit chagrined, as I thought my dealings with Nellie Fry were such that her brother would have asked me to do the legal work. A year later I met him at a community function and I brought up the subject. He said "Oh, it never occurred to me to ask you. I just thought that Charlie Adams had more experience in estates and that I should go to him." That kind of frustration is typical for a young lawyer.

In 1966 I was walking down the same hallway in the Addison County Courthouse when Judge Sylvester stopped me. A few weeks earlier I had successfully defended my first homicide in a case involving a young boy, who while defending his brother from some physical abuse, had shot and killed his father. That case was tried in St. Albans, in Franklin County. Judge Sylvester lived in St. Albans, and I am sure he was well aware of the families involved. He said, "Peter, I read about the acquittal of the Gibson boy up in Franklin County. Tell me, was your client really guilty?" I was taken aback. I stammered, not knowing exactly how to answer. Suddenly, a smile came across the judge's face, and he said, "The jury said he wasn't, and that's all that matters." He walked away chuckling to himself.

Jury verdicts in Vermont both in criminal and civil cases must be unanimous. After a jury has rendered its verdict, the court always asks, "Is that the verdict of all of you?" There is a generalized response of "yes," and the court then turns to the losing lawyer and asks if that attorney wishes to have the jury polled. Some lawyers do have the jury polled, and some lawyers don't. I always do, perhaps mostly out of a sense of frustration and wanting each one of the jurors to have to take home with them the responsibility for the judgment they have made against my client. However, every once in a while lightning strikes.

In the late 1960s, I was defending a case of careless and negligent driving before the Honorable Hilton "Spike" Dier. On the panel of jurors was Mrs. Munson. At one time I had successfully represented her husband in a trespass case against Harry Goodro.[7] The Munsons were an old-time Middlebury family, but they did not have the economic clout of Goodro, who was a prominent citizen and the owner of Goodro's Lumber Yard in East Middlebury. I had also represented Mrs. Munson's sons concerning various escapades that they had gotten into, and I had even prosecuted one of them when I was state's attorney. Based on my experience, I couldn't believe that Mrs. Munson would ever convict anybody of anything.

The jury was out for a considerable period of time, considering the nature of the case, and finally came back with a guilty verdict. Mrs. Munson was the No. 11 juror. After the judge inquired of the jury if this was the verdict of all of them, he looked at me and said, "Mr. Langrock, would you like the jury polled?" Upon my affirmative response, he had the clerk read the name of each of the jurors. The response of the first juror was "guilty." The same question was asked of each juror and each responded "guilty," until the clerk came to the eleventh juror. She crossed her arms in front of her and responded, "Not guilty."

Spike Dier, who had been treating this as the most routine of matters, suddenly jerked alert and said to the foreman, "Mr. Foreman, I thought you had reached a unanimous verdict." The foreman responded, "I thought we had, too!" Spike said, "I'm going to send you back into the jury room to make a determination of where we are." He then excused the jury. I immediately approached the bench and called for a mistrial. Spike looked at me, smiled, and said, "We'll see what the jury does first." Five minutes later, the jurors filed back out once again with a verdict of guilty. This time, upon individual questioning, even juror No. 11 said "guilty." The bailiff later told me that as he was standing outside the jury room he heard a loud argument which concluded when Mrs. Munson finally shouted, "All right, all right, I'm sorry I said it." The judge took care of any possibility of an appeal by fining my client fifty dollars rather than imposing a jail sentence.

When I was sworn in as state's attorney, in 1960, the Addison County sheriff was Morton Coons. His son, Jim Coons, is the sheriff today. Mort had been a state police officer and had left that service to run for sheriff. He later became an assistant judge, and as such he exercised control not only from the bench, but over the maintenance of the court buildings. Usually, rather than hiring outside help, he took care of the maintenance personally. In addition, Mort and his wife Betty ran the Addison County Jail on the east side of Court Street. The jail was used for holding people who were awaiting trial and who had not made bail, and also for people with relatively short sentences. There was one "permanent-regular" resident, Fletcher McIntyre, who had a drinking problem. Whenever he was released from jail, he would get drunk and immediately be returned to the jail. Over the years there evolved a pattern. Fletch would be sentenced to serve ninety days for drunk and disorderly conduct, would go to jail, spend his ninety days there, be released from jail, promptly get drunk, and the next day he would be back in for another ninety-day sentence.

This would not seem unusual, except that Sheriff Coons gave Fletch what was called "the liberties of the jail yard." This meant that the prisoner could leave the jail as he pleased, go into town, and do whatever was necessary from his point of view. Fletch's only real duties were to keep the jail clean. The fascinating thing was that Fletch would no more have a drink when he had the liberties of the jail yard than he would commit a serious crime. But as soon as he was released from jail and was not on a trustee status, he immediately went back to the bottle.

On one particular occasion, after Fletch's fifth or sixth ninety-day stretch since my taking on the office of state's attorney, he was riding in an automobile while completely ossified. The passenger-side door opened and Fletch rolled out of the car, which was traveling at forty or fifty miles per hour. Thanks to his alcohol consumption, he was in a totally relaxed state. He simply rolled and rolled, and he survived with only some minor scraping and bruising. A sober man would probably have been killed. This incident gave rise to another charge of public intoxication, which would allow him to spend the next ninety days in jail.

When he arrived in court on Saturday morning for arraignment on the charge, we thought we would have a little fun with him. As the court read the charge against him, I rose and addressed the court. "Your Honor, I think that we have a serious problem on our hands by way of recidivism. Mr. McIntyre has been an inhabitant of the jail, returning there every ninety days, for the past twenty or twenty-five years. Given the dangerous condition of his falling out of the car, I suggest that Mr. McIntyre has a mental problem and that he should be examined at the state hospital in Waterbury." Fletch thought he was being double-crossed and immediately jumped up saying, "I'm not crazy. I just need to get back into jail." He looked over at me, I withdrew my request for observation at Waterbury, and Fletch went back to his ninety-day jail routine.

As an aside, Fletch was an accomplished clock repairer and he could take any old traditional watch or clock and turn it into a finely tuned chronometer. He eventually lived out his natural life in the Addison County Jail and passed away there, somewhere in the neighborhood of seventy years of age.

One of the most important pieces of furniture in my office in the northeast corner of the courthouse was an enamel spittoon. Working in the office next to George Farr, the county clerk, and also having clerked with Wynn Underwood, both ardent tobacco chewers, I resumed the habit which I had first tried as a teenager. One Saturday morning I got to my office early, and with the door open I was reviewing the files for the municipal court hearings that day, which were scheduled for eleven o'clock. I was wearing my best and only three-piece suit, with a chew going, and my feet on the desk, in a position from which, by moving only my head, I had relatively easy access to the spittoon.

Into this scene walked a gentleman from Rhode Island. Upon inquiry, he said that he had come to answer charges of careless driving. Three weeks before he had gone off the road on Route 7 in New Haven and had received a court citation. Rather than paying a fine by mail, he had returned to Vermont to explain his situation, as he believed he hadn't done anything wrong. I asked him what had happened, and he described passing a line of cars when one of them pulled out without notice, forcing his vehicle onto the far shoulder. The shoulder was soft, causing him to go off the road and into the field. I picked up the phone and called Al Ghio, the investigating state trooper (who later served a term as sheriff), and I explained the Rhode Islander's position to him. Al told me, "It probably could have happened that way." Without moving my feet from the desk, I hung up the phone and told the fellow, "I'm going to dismiss your case. We appreciate your coming to Vermont and we want you to have a feeling that Vermont treats people fairly." He appeared a bit taken aback. In his hand he had a ballpoint pen which advertised his Rhode Island business. Since he didn't know what else to say, he asked, "Can I give you this pen?" I looked at the pen, which had a value of probably thirty or forty cents, and I replied, "I guess that's all right." I took the pen and was careful to use it only on state business.

I still have a mental image of that man going back to his home in Rhode Island and saying, "You won't believe what happened to me today! I walked in and saw a young man in his early twenties dressed in a three-piece suit, chewing tobacco, with his legs up on a desk—and who, without moving, made a phone call and then dismissed the charges against me."

9. The International Paper Company

The International Paper Company litigation touched the Addison County Courthouse for only a short while, but it affected the community, the county, and the state of Vermont in many ways.

This story begins during the reign of our current U.S. Senator, Jim Jeffords, as attorney general, and it takes place under the command of his deputy attorney general, Fred I. Parker. In the mid-1960s, the state became concerned that the paper mill at Ticonderoga in New York State, which had been owned and operated by International Paper since 1925, had been dumping sludge left over from the paper-making process into Ticonderoga Bay. This sludge had formed a bed in the bay which was encroaching on the channel of the southern portion of Lake Champlain known as the

South Lake. As the dividing line between the state of New York and Vermont was the deepest point of the channel, the effect of the encroachment of this sludge bed was to alter the interstate boundary, so that the state of New York actually became bigger and the state of Vermont smaller.

In December of 1970, the state of Vermont filed an action against the state of New York directly in the United States Supreme Court, under the provision giving that Court original and exclusive jurisdiction in disputes between states. The suit alleged that New York had failed to abate the papermill's pollution, and it named International Paper as an additional party. In order to determine the relevant facts in the dispute, the Supreme Court appointed R. Ami Cutter, the former chief justice of the Commonwealth of Massachusetts and later the president of the American Law Institute, as its "master" to hear the evidence in the case and report back to the court on his findings.

Besides Deputy Attorney General Parker, other assistant attorneys general played a major role in the development of the case. One of those, Jim Morse, now serves on the Vermont Supreme Court, and another was a brilliant—if sometimes contentious—Middlebury native by the name of John Calhoun. (The same John Calhoun as represented Wayne Bosworth on appeal—Chapter III.)

Before the master undertook his duties, there was an oral argument in the U.S. Supreme Court on the question of whether the state had set out sufficient facts for the court to take jurisdiction. Arguing for International Paper was Taggart Whipple of the large and somewhat pompous New York law firm, Davis, Polk & Wardwell. Arguing for the state of Vermont was Fred Parker. At one point during the oral argument, Taggart Whipple held up to the Court a picture-postcard of Ticonderoga Bay, site of the sludge bed. He quoted a passage from Thomas Jefferson, writing about his visits to Lake George and how the river running into the south lake had always been a muddy, undesirable waterway. Whipple argued that, in effect, the paper mill had not in any way adversely affected this muddy water as depicted on the beautiful picture-postcard. Justice Douglas could no longer contain himself. He leaned over the Supreme Court bench, looked at Taggart Whipple, and said, "Mr. Whipple, you make this sludge bed sound so attractive, perhaps every lake should have one!" The Court determined there was jurisdiction and the trial began before the master.

The master took evidence from experts on both sides. Three of

Vermont's most stalwart authorities on contamination issues were the scientists Carl Pagel, Dave Folger, and Dick Haupt. Carl and David worked for the Vermont Department of Fish & Wildlife, while Dick was on loan from Vermont's Department of Transportation. In preparing for their testimony, they donned diving suits and actively inspected the lake floor to see what was happening first-hand. They studied the degradation to the microorganisms living on the lake floor, and they mapped the size and scope of the sludge bed. In large part due to their findings, and after many days of grueling testimony, the case finally resulted in a tripartite settlement. Among other things, the settlement called for the closing of the old paper mill, the building of a (supposedly) pollution-free new mill, and the establishment of a $500,000 trust paid for by International Paper, to protect the South Lake (supposedly) and to be administered by the state of Vermont. The trust's last assets were subsequently squandered on a weed harvest program to replace funds from the state of Vermont's general fund.

While this was happening, another facet of the litigation got underway. Early one October morning in 1971, H. Keith Zahn, a former Boeing aircraft engineer from Kansas—and a person of sufficient ability and character to be worthy of a book himself—was sitting in a duck blind at Owl's Head Harbor on the eastern (Vermont) shore of the lake. Keith had left Boeing to grow apples in Vermont. I happened to have the privilege of being his hunting companion that morning as we looked over a string of decoys for incoming whistlers. A light wind started blowing up the lake from the south. Although we were approximately twenty miles north of the Ticonderoga mill, the sulfur smell emitted from the mill was evident and obnoxious as we sat there waiting for a flight of ducks. Recognizing the smell, Keith said, "You know, there must be something we can do about this." I suggested that if he was willing to go forward, we could investigate the possibility of bringing a class action for the landowners on the Vermont side of the lake. He thought that was a good idea.

While the unpleasant smell coming from the mill was the catalyst for this class action litigation, Keith Zahn was even better acquainted with the other problems caused by the mill's emissions. His orchard, in Orwell, had more than a half-mile of lake frontage, almost directly across from Ticonderoga Bay and the mill. His family was often faced with the mill's malodorous air emissions and, when he walked on his lakefront property, the water pollution from the mill coloring the water, as well as flotsam breaking off from the sludge bed, was apparent as well. The air emissions were of sufficient potency and the wind currents were such that at times the noxious odors from the mill could even be smelled in the village of Middlebury, inland and over twenty miles away.

Keith and his wife, Valerie, who later went on to get her law degree, met with their good friends, Charlie and Marion Leazer, owners of a boat marina in Orwell, to discuss the possibility of a suit. The Leazers were interested and asked if they could join as parties to the lawsuit. Charlie Leazer told stories of chunks of black flotsam which had obviously broken off from the sludge pile, floating up, and contaminating his docks and shores. He told of the smelly and murky water, and of the rotten-cabbage-like sulphur smell from the mill.

It appeared that we had enough facts to go forward with the class action. What we were short on were funds to finance expert witnesses who would be needed to testify at trial. I approached Attorney General Jim Jeffords with the idea of bringing the class action on behalf of all the Vermont lakeshore owners. I asked him if he would make available to us the expertise that the state had put together in its case before the United States Supreme Court. Jim, a strong environmentalist, was concerned about the impact on Lake Champlain and on the lakeshore landowners, and he readily promised to help. That promise was essential to our private litigation. Fortunately for the property owners, after Jim went on to represent Vermont in Congress, his successor Attorneys General continued to honor it.

Zahn v. International Paper Company was brought in the United States District Court for the District of Vermont. To no one's surprise, the firm of Davis, Polk & Wardwell was engaged to defend International Paper. Davis, Polk's local counsel was Henry Black, of Black & Plante in White River Junction. Henry had been a Vermont superior judge early in his career, and although he had returned to private practice, he was still known as Judge Black. His renown as a fine advocate was built on some wonderful verdicts in condemnation cases when the state was building the interstate highway system; on his work as a lobbyist in the state legislature against a bill requiring a deposit on beer and soda containers; and on his generally exceptional abilities as a trial lawyer. All of this made him a sound choice for the role of the mill's Vermont counsel. Henry later served as a member of the Board of Governors of the American

Bar Association, and in fact he died from a heart attack while attending a session of that board. One personal debt I owe to Henry is that he taught me to drink Jack Daniels Manhattans straight up.

The first round of the class-action litigation took place in U.S. District Judge Bernard Leddy's chambers. Henry Black was there in his usual cordial manner, and so was Taggart Whipple, who personified the stiff New York lawyer. Whipple held all plaintiffs' lawyers in contempt, especially those who would dare to challenge his client, International Paper Company. The atmosphere was rather tense as we were ushered into chambers, in contrast to the friendly attitude which was the norm among Vermont lawyers. Whipple acknowledged me with a cold stare and a nod of his head.

Judge Leddy questioned me quite thoroughly to determine that we were able to prepare this case responsibly as a serious piece of litigation. He wanted to ensure that this was not simply a strike suit, which is an action brought in an attempt to exact a quick settlement based solely on the threat of litigation and the costs of defense. This was a reasonable inquiry, as our firm at that time was small, consisting only of Mark Sperry and myself. In addition, Rule 23 of the Federal Rules of Civil Procedure, which governs class actions, requires that the judge inquire both as to the ability of the named plaintiffs to represent the interests of the class and also as to the capabilities of the lawyers bringing the action. I explained to the court that we understood that extensive resources would be required to pursue the claims in the suit, and that the firm contemplated hiring an associate to work on the case if necessary.

Apparently satisfied, the judge leaned back in his chair and looked at Taggart Whipple. Mr. Whipple took off his reading glasses and, using them as a prop, proceeded to suggest that a class action was not appropriate and that we were impertinent to even think of bringing such a case. After a few minutes, Judge Leddy leaned further back in his chair, paused a moment, and then indicated that he thought this was in fact just the type of situation in which a class action was appropriate. He indicated, however, that he would have to consider it more thoroughly and would shortly thereafter issue a written decision. On hearing Judge Leddy's comment, Whipple, who had replaced his glasses after finishing his presentation, reached up and snatched them off again, preparing to reargue his position. Before he could speak, the judge ended the chambers hearing, leaving Whipple with a dazed look.

Whipple had represented a Connecticut company, Scovill Brass, where Mark Sperry's father had been an officer. He approached Mark after the hearing, as a courtesy or out of curiosity, to inquire if he were related to Mark L. Sperry II, of Scovill. Mark acknowledged the relationship and then attempted to introduce me to Whipple. I extended my right hand to shake Whipple's. Very reluctantly, as shown by his body language, he shook my hand. I simply smiled. Our relationship never got much better.

A month later we got the written decision from Judge Leddy.[8] Much to our surprise, he said that although he thought a class action would be the appropriate vehicle to help remedy the harm being done to the lake, he did not have jurisdictional authority to authorize a class action. This was based on the legal proposition that not every member of the class could individually claim the $10,000 minimum in damages required for jurisdiction in the federal court system. Although the suit had also sought punitive damages, by charging that International Paper's actions were in wanton and reckless disregard of the rights of the Vermont lakeshore owners—and although with such punitive damages each class member's claim exceeded $10,000—somehow this legal issue got lost in the shuffle. Unfortunately, the issue of punitive damages as a basis for class-action jurisdiction continued to be lost in the shuffle all the way to the U.S. Supreme Court.

We requested an interlocutory appeal from Judge Leddy's order, which would allow us immediate appellate review of the legal issues. We wanted the case to proceed as a class action, with the clout of two hundred landowners, before turning to prepare for trial. The requested appeal was to the United States Court of Appeals for the Second Circuit, which hears cases from Vermont, Connecticut, and New York. An interlocutory appeal requires the appellate court's permission before it can be heard. Our request for such an appeal was granted. Usually oral arguments are heard in the federal courthouse in Foley Square in Manhattan, near where the Brooklyn Bridge joins Manhattan. In a rare diversion from that practice, Mark Sperry, who had prepared the briefs, argued the case before a three-judge panel sitting in New Haven, Connecticut. A short time later we were informed that by a two-to-one decision, the panel upheld Judge Leddy's decision.[9] Judge William H. Timbers dissented.

Based upon this dissent, we prepared a motion for reargument "en banc," asking for the entire second circuit court, rather than just a three-judge panel, to sit, hear arguments, and then decide the case. There were nine seats on the second circuit court of appeals, but only seven were currently filled. The decision of the seven judges was split, with four agreeing there was jurisdiction for a class action, and three saying there was no jurisdiction. Although at first blush this appeared to be a win, five of the seven sitting judges took the further position that a majority of the entire court, or five out of nine votes, was required to overrule the panel. Thus, by the five-to-two vote, the seven decided a four-to-three vote was insufficient to grant class-action status. This decision remains today one of the leading opinions dealing with "en banc" appeals in the second circuit.[10]

Just about this time, Richard B. "Ben" Hirst, a recent Harvard Law School graduate, had accepted a clerkship with U.S. District Judge James Holden, who had been appointed to the federal bench after serving for several years as chief justice of the Vermont Supreme Court. Ben had a period of about three months between his graduation from law school and his assumption of the clerkship, and he was looking for short-term employment. He had applied at the attorney general's office and talked to Fred Parker, who was prepared to offer him a job. At that time Fred had already decided to leave the attorney general's office to join our firm. Not knowing this, Ben decided to walk into our office "cold," without an appointment. Although we had no clerkship position open, I agreed to interview him, more out of curiosity than anything else. He was so bright and personable that within ten minutes I offered him a job. He accepted our offer over a position at the attorney general's office.

Ben's first assignment was to prepare a writ of certiorari to the United States Supreme Court seeking an appeal of the second circuit decision. The U.S. Supreme Court grants a hearing for only one hundred of the more than four thousand requests for certiorari that are made each year. Surprisingly, Ben's efforts were successful, and the petition for certiorari was granted. That was the beginning of a very auspicious career for Ben, who later became the general counsel of Northwest Airlines.

The day we received word that the U.S. Supreme Court had granted certiorari, I called up Henry Black: "Henry, I just heard that the Supreme Court granted certiorari in the International Paper case." Ever congenial, Henry responded with excitement: "Oh, that's good." Then he focused on the fact that we had been the petitioner, and added: "Well, I guess it's not." I said, "Henry, you made your first fortune on the bottle bill, the second on interstate condemnation cases, and this one is going to be your third." We laughed and started looking forward to our trip to Washington.

My partner, Jon Stahl, prepared the brief for the Supreme Court. Jon was a graduate of Columbia Law School and interviewed with me upon his graduation in 1965. Because it looked as though he was about to be drafted, I hired another young man who was married and less likely to be drafted. Such a decision would probably be illegal today under our employment-discrimination laws. Jon joined the FBI, and after four years with the bureau, he returned to Vermont to become an assistant attorney general. While at the attorney general's office, Jon agreed to join our firm and eventually it was he who convinced Fred Parker to leave the attorney general's office and join us.

International Paper filed its brief and the matter was set for oral argument before the full court in Washington. When the time came, the Supreme Court notified us that our case was the fifth on its docket for that particular week. The Court hears arguments in four cases each day. Nonetheless, as the fifth case, we had to be present in Court on that Monday, in the event one of the four ahead of us did not use its full time. If that happened, we would be expected to start our argument on Monday afternoon. As it turned out, the first four cases went as scheduled, and the Court adjourned on Monday afternoon.

In the hall outside the courtroom, I was visiting with Dick Nolan, a younger partner from Davis Polk working on the case. Dick was a true gentleman. While fitting the mold of a New York lawyer, he was anything but pompous. Taggart Whipple, who was actually going to argue the next day, came over to say something to Nolan, who then attempted to introduce Whipple to me. Although I had not seen Whipple since that day in Judge Leddy's chambers, I had not forgotten him. Apparently, he had forgotten me, and he simply mumbled: "Oh, it's nice to meet you." After Whipple left, I told Dick that I hoped Whipple's memory was better on the morrow than it appeared to be that afternoon.

Having argued many cases in the Vermont Supreme Court, I attempted to be rather blasé about the upcoming event. The truth of the matter is that any argument before the U.S. Supreme Court is a very exciting and daunting experience.

The next morning I arrived at Court and sat at the petitioner's table on the left side of the podium facing the bench. I was there by myself, with no supporting staff. I hadn't even invited friends or family members to watch the argument. Looking back, I don't think I fully appreciated the significance of arguing a case before the U.S. Supreme Court. At defense table there were Taggart Whipple, Dick Nolan, Henry Black, and, seated directly behind them, a number of associates ready to pick up any index cards that Taggart Whipple discarded back over his shoulder in their direction. After swearing in some new members to the Supreme Court Bar, Chief Justice Warren Burger nodded to me and I commenced my half-hour argument.

Appellate judges often state that oral arguments seldom make a difference in their decision of a case. I expect that was true in this case, and this was not one of my better appellate arguments. When Justice White quizzed me on a particular holding in a case we had cited in our brief, I blanked out on the details of the case. Only after my argument was finished and I sat down again at counsel table did it become clear to me that his questions indicated he would probably side against us in the decision.

One truly joyous moment of that oral argument came when Taggart Whipple suggested that a particular U.S. Supreme Court precedent applied, and consistency required the court to affirm the lower court's decision. Justice Douglas questioned him about the precedent, and Whipple's response was that Justice Douglas had dissented in that very case, and that his dissent indicated that the majority holding would be binding in this case. Justice Douglas sat back, smiled, and chortled, "Well, you know us dissenters, we sometimes overstate our position."

After the Supreme Court voted six-to—three against our position,[11] the matter was remanded to the Vermont District Court for pretrial proceedings as an ordinary civil case on behalf of Zahn and Leazer alone, and not as a class action. We were greatly disappointed with the majority opinion, though not surprised. This was a period when the Burger court was concerned about the number of cases over which the federal courts had jurisdiction. This decision would prevent large numbers of consumers with only modest claims from joining together in a class to look to the federal court system for relief, thus lightening the workload of the federal courts.

However, as the Zahn and Leazer claims were still alive, including our claim for punitive damages, we still had a good case to go forward with. The first three years of the litigation had dealt only with procedural matters. Now discovery would begin, with the examination of the facts surrounding the mill's pollution practices and the impacts on the Zahn and Leazer properties.

During discovery, we gathered information about the sludge bed and the history of the operation of the old mill. We found that the old mill had been shut down during the three years of preliminary litigation and that the lake in the area of Ticonderoga Bay was recovering at a rate that surprised everyone. The two individual claims were relatively modest, and our best hope for a substantial verdict would be punitive damages. Punitive damages, while not being considered by the court for class certification, could still be awarded to Zahn and Leazer for intentional wrongdoing, or reckless and wanton conduct. A hearing was set for the first week in September, 1975, to determine whether we had sufficient evidence to go forward on our punitive damage claim. I had little doubt that we could prove the mill's emissions had caused air and water pollution. However, International Paper's operations were consistent with industry practice at the time, and it was a real question as to whether the facts would sustain a verdict on punitive damages.

Prior to the September meeting, a meeting was set for settlement discussions at Henry Black's office in White River Junction. New York counsel came up for the meeting, having indicated they were prepared to make a proposal for a settlement. Fred Parker, by then my partner and well acquainted with the opposition from his work on the state's boundary case, joined me for the meeting. We decided to set up a "tough guy—easygoing guy" scenario. Fred, who is 6'5" and at least 250 pounds, but possessed of the gentlest demeanor, was to play the tough guy. I, who tend to be much more volatile and usually rise to the fly as soon as it is thrown upon the water, agreed to play against type as the easygoing guy.

We arrived and, after the niceties were exchanged, International Paper's attorneys put a sum of money on the table as a possible settlement. It was a low sum. Without even thinking, I slammed my briefcase shut, told them their offer was an insult and, in proper tough guy fashion started to walk out. Parker, suddenly deprived of his prearranged role as the tough guy, had no choice but to placate me and keep the discussion going. Nevertheless, we made no further progress that day, and finally we both got up and left. As we walked down the stairs, we burst out laughing: neither one of us had been able to change our spots, and our attempt to switch roles had been a complete failure.

Often in late summer I can be found driving harness horses in races at the various fairs around the state. The Champlain Valley Fair in Essex Junction had a three-day race meet which was then the best competition in the state. The meet was held the week before Labor Day, 1975. Our hearing on the applicability of punitive damages was scheduled the next week before Judge Albert Coffrin, Judge Leddy having passed away since our initial hearing on the case four years earlier.

If we were going to settle the case, the best chance to settle it was before that hearing. Once the die was cast on the question of punitive damages, whatever leverage each party had would be gone, and there would be a higher likelihood of proceeding to trial. As the first race was called onto the track, the loudspeaker called me to the phone at the racing office on the back stretch of the Essex Junction Fairgrounds. It was Dick Nolan. For the next few hours I kept that phone busy, between races, with calls to my office, to Dick Nolan, and to the clients. Somewhere between the fifth and sixth race we reached a settlement of the case. Although the actual settlement remains confidential, it can be said both that our clients received generous payments and that IPC got off lightly, considering the extent of the pollution its mill had caused.

That is not, however, the end of the International Paper story. A couple of years later, Harmel Ouellette called up early one morning and asked if he could come see me. Harmel operated a top-flight dairy farm located on the Vermont shores of Lake Champlain. He is also a Vermonter whose family came from Quebec, and he speaks with a French-Canadian accent. He walked into my office and said, "Peter, I wake up this morning, get out of bed, and there is this awful stink. I think my wife she fart in bed and I go outside and find it is the f——ing paper company. Can't we do something about this?" Thus started *Ouellette v. International Paper Company*, and the connection of this case to the Addison County Courthouse.

After meeting with me, Harmel had spoken with a number of his fellow lakeshore property owners, and there was great interest in bringing another suit against International Paper Company. We decided to go forward with a second nuisance action, this time against the operation of International Paper's new mill. We also determined to seek class-action status for all owners of lakeshore land in the towns of Shoreham, Bridport, and Addison, the three Vermont towns across the lake from the mill, and also all the residents of those same three towns.

Being fully aware of the jurisdictional problems we had encountered in federal court in *Zahn*, we brought this case in the Addison Superior Court. The suit was greeted with great fanfare by the press, and the courthouse staff looked forward to a really interesting piece of litigation. Much to their chagrin, however, as International Paper did not wish to try this case before an Addison County jury or state-court judges, by filing papers in federal court, they had the case transferred from the Addison County Court to the U.S. District Court for the District of Vermont. Then, International Paper immediately moved to dismiss the class action on the same grounds alleged in *Zahn*: that not every member of the class could meet the $10,000 jurisdictional amount. The case was assigned to Judge Coffrin, who indicated quite clearly that they could not have it both ways: they could not take the case out of state court demanding federal jurisdiction and then try to dismiss the case because the U.S. District Court lacked federal jurisdiction. Moreover, we had requested injunctive relief on behalf of the class, seeking an order prohibiting the mill from discharging polluted water into the lake. The court determined that, based on the potential costs to the mill if the relief were granted, the value of this claim clearly met the jurisdictional limit. In addition, the suit claimed punitive damages on behalf of the class, giving the court a second basis for finding federal court jurisdiction.

Initially, we attempted to certify to two classes: one for lakefront owners on the Vermont shores of Lake Champlain, who were affected by water and air pollution; the other for the residents of the towns of Shoreham, Bridport, and Addison, affected only by the air pollution. Judge Coffrin originally allowed the first class, but he denied certification of the second class, ruling that it was too difficult to define a class based on diffuse claims of air pollution over such a large geographic area. Later, Judge Coffrin included the air-pollution claims in the class of waterfront owners. Thus we were permitted to proceed with a class-action lawsuit for air and water pollution on behalf of all Vermont lakefront owners in the towns of Shoreham, Bridport and Addison, south of the Crown Point Bridge.

We were ordered to prepare a list of all potential class members, from the towns' real-property tax records. The court then sent out notices to the class, describing the class-action claims. Class members were told that if they did not want to be included, they could return an enclosed postcard, indicating their desire to opt out of the class. Of approximately 220 potential class members, almost one-third did opt out, leaving a class of approximately 150 lakeshore owners.

Fairly soon in the proceeding, Jim Benkard, one of the third round of Davis, Polk attorneys in the IPC case, filed a motion to dismiss the suit. International Paper now argued that the Federal Clean Water Act of 1972 preempted the rights of private citizens to bring a nuisance action involving pollution of interstate waters. This issue had been raised in another Federal court case, *Illinois v. Milwaukee*, which arose out of pollution in Lake Michigan. That case had already worked its way to the Supreme Court on two earlier occasions, and was now awaiting a decision by the Court of Appeals for the Seventh Circuit. Judge Coffrin decided to take the motion in our case under advisement until the seventh circuit issued its decision. Unfortunately, it was almost three years later, in 1985, before the seventh circuit acted, and its eventual decision was adverse to our position. Nevertheless, Judge Coffrin disagreed with their decision, and, deciding he was not bound by it, he denied International Paper's motion to dismiss.[12]

International Paper filed an application for an interlocutory appeal to the second circuit, the permission was granted. After the usual rounds of briefing and oral arguments, the second circuit agreed with Judge Coffrin and affirmed his ruling, paving the way back to Vermont Federal District Court for trial.[13] International Paper, however, had other ideas, and petitioned for a writ of certiorari in the United States Supreme Court.

Interestingly, on the way from the Second Circuit to the Supreme Court, International Paper replaced its long-time attorneys, Davis, Polk & Wardwell, with another prestigious New York firm: Simpson, Thatcher & Bartlett, whose chief litigator was Roy Reardon. We could only surmise that International Paper was dissatisfied with the way the Vermont litigation had been handled, and sought new blood. We later learned International Paper had a new in-house counsel who had formerly practiced law at Simpson, Thatcher.

Oral argument was set for November 4, 1986. Three days before heading off to Washington, the entire firm met in our library to prepare me for oral argument. Such mock practices are called "moot court." All the attorneys asked questions as tough as any I could expect from the Supreme Court. Two days later Emily Joselson, my partner who had prepared the written brief, I, our spouses, and several of our clients took off for the nation's capital. Our entourage was in contrast to my blasé attitude of my first trip to the Supreme Court.

The day before the oral argument, we met with Lawrence G.

Wallace of the Solicitor General's Office. The United States had entered the case in support of our position that the Clean-Water Act did not pre-empt a private cause/action. I had agreed to share my half-hour of oral argument with the Solicitor's Office, so I had only fifteen minutes to argue. Assistant Solicitor Wallace was given our other fifteen minutes. We met to divide the responsibilities of our arguments, so that we could make best use of the half-hour allotted. Lawrence Wallace was the most experienced assistant solicitor general in the office at that time. He told us this was going to be his eighty-seventh argument before the Court. At the Solicitor's Office, I underwent my second moot court grilling.

On the day of argument, Emily and I arrived at Court early, as we were scheduled to be the first of the four arguments. On entering the courthouse we met Roy Reardon, who was scheduled to argue the case for International Paper. One of the small joys for me in this litigation was to be the small-town lawyer from Middlebury, Vermont, who, having argued in the Supreme Court before, knew the lay of the land, knew where the clerk's office was, knew the general procedures for getting ready for the argument and, most important, knew where the men's room was. I had the pleasure of showing off this knowledge to Roy Reardon, the senior litigator from one of the biggest and most prestigious law firms in the country, as he was a first-timer in the Supreme Court.

I was dressed in my best dark suit and felt quite presentable, but my appearance paled next to that of Lawrence Wallace. As is the tradition, the lawyers from the U.S. Solicitor's Office always appear in morning coats when arguing before the Supreme Court. After the nine judges filed onto the bench, the first order of the day was the admission of new members to the Supreme Court bar. I had the pleasure of moving the admission of my partner, Emily Joselson, as well as Meredith Wright, an assistant attorney general from Vermont, who had come down to watch the argument. Meredith, a fellow alumnus of the University of Chicago, later became the first environmental judge in Vermont's judicial system.

The oral arguments went reasonably well. At least this time I did not feel I had left wide-open questions or failed to respond appropriately to the Court's inquiries. As soon as our argument was over, we exited at the rear of the courtroom, leaving just as the second argument of the day was getting underway. We started walking down the long hall towards the steps leading from the front door of the Supreme Court to the street. Emily didn't say a single word to me until we got halfway down the often-photographed front steps of the Supreme Court. There she finally acknowledged that she thought the argument had gone well. We all relaxed, at last, over lunch at a gourmet restaurant, with appropriate libations, before heading home.

A little over two months later we got the word that we had won—by a 9-0 vote—the important legal ruling that a private right of action was preserved under the Clean Water Act. However, International Paper prevailed by a 5-4 vote on the subsidiary issue that New York's nuisance law governed the controversy. With the legal issues clearly resolved, we were now headed back to the trial court.[14] Our attention was now focused on whether we would be able to prove our factual allegations at trial.

The discovery process was long and arduous. Emily Joselson and Roy Reardon got along just like Sitting Bull and General Custer. Depositions of even relatively minor witnesses became hard-fought and emotionally draining.

The certified class included all landowners on the east side of the lake, from the southern border of Shoreham to the Crown Point toll bridge between Addison and New York. International Paper attempted to prove that the odor from the mill could not possibly affect landowners as far north as the bridge. They employed an engineering firm from Connecticut to conduct a study to prove just that. The study's protocol consisted of engineers going to the mill and, with a vacuum jug, capturing the air emissions from the smokestacks at International Paper. The engineers went down to the Lake George area and hired fifteen people off the unemployment rolls. These fifteen persons were given a sniffing test. The three people who had the least sensitive noses and the three with the most sensitive noses were dismissed. Thus, International Paper's engineers were left with a panel of nine mediocre sniffers. The panel of sniffers was then herded into a room and furnished with face masks. Into the masks was first pumped the clean sweet air of Lake George. Slowly, the clean air was mixed with increasing amounts of emissions from the stacks at IPC. These emissions were gradually increased until they were first detected, and continued until a point where the odor could be identified. The concentrations necessary for detection and identification were duly noted by the engineers. The Connecticut firm also conducted a thorough study of the wind currents in the area between the mill and the Vermont class members' properties. Based upon the air-current study and the carefully calibrated findings of the nine mediocre sniffers, the mill's engineering firm opined that it was impossible for the landowners near the Crown Point Bridge to smell air emissions discharged from the mill.

In the meantime, we prepared our counter-evidence. We interviewed the toll-takers at the Crown Point Bridge, who had worked there for decades. Their testimony was simple and unanimous: whenever there was a south wind, coming from the direction of the mill, people from out-of-state would roll down their windows, stop their cars and say, "What the hell is that awful smell?" We didn't have consulting companies or professional sniffers, but there was no doubt that we had the better of the argument. It is rumored that the next assignment this engineering company took on was to prove that bumblebees cannot fly.

We arranged for the return of the wonderful team of experts who had been the backbone witnesses for the State of Vermont in its original case against the old mill: Carl Pagel, still working for the Vermont Department of Fish & Wildlife; Dick Haupt, still with Vermont's Department of Transportation; and Dave Folger, who was now at the Woods Hole Oceanographic Institute. Haupt and Fogel made a series of new dives into the south lake to update their studies with data on the impact of the new mill's water discharges on the lake bottom. Pagel examined the microorganisms living on the lake bottom. They verified what we had seen in aerial color photographs: polluted sludge from the mill's wastewater-treatment plant was being pumped through an underwater pipe and discharged within a thousand feet of the New York-Vermont border. This resulted in a plume of contamination spreading out from the mill's discharge pipe.

We had four additional experts: James Morris, an industrial engineer from the University of Vermont; Jeffrey Laible, a UVM civil engineer; UVM fisheries expert George LaBar; and a wonderful man from New York City, Amos Turk, who was our air-pollution specialist. Amos had been involved in the design of many water-treatment plants in New York City. Not only were his credentials unimpeachable, but he had an engaging sense of humor—and a great sense of smell.

One other discovery story of note was that IPC had hired a water treatment expert who was teaching at Miami University in Ohio. I journeyed out to Ohio to take his deposition. Appearing for Simpson, Thatcher and Bartlett was a partner who was new to the case and who had very little knowledge of the facts. Their experts started to testify in ways that were quite favorable to our side of the case. In his opinion, there was technology available to clean up the effluent completely before discharging it into Lake Champlain, although he waffled on the cost of that technology. Suddenly, IPC's attorney instructed the expert not to answer any more questions and ended the deposition.

I returned from Ohio and we headed to court to seek an order requiring the expert to answer my questions. The court granted our motion, but by that time the expert had left the country and was in a boat off the North Atlantic coast. He was scheduled to be in port for one day only. We arranged to finish his deposition by telephone on that day. I sat in our office in Middlebury while the expert was seated by a phone in Boston, accompanied by his lawyer. Everybody was expecting a lengthy continuation of the deposition. After the preliminaries, I simply asked whether it was, in fact, technologically possible for the mill's water discharges to be completely purified before they entered the lake. His answer was "yes." I decided not to try to gild the lily, and said, "No more questions." Does a one-question deposition qualify for *The Guinness Book of World Records?*

As discovery closed and the trial date approached, serious discussions about a settlement commenced. I went to New York and had dinner with Roy Reardon, during which we finally got down to brass tacks. I told him I was looking forward to trying the case. I suggested that a Vermont jury would be sympathetic to us, and that we expected a large compensatory verdict for the damages that were caused by the mill's pollution. In addition, we had a real shot at punitive damages, given International Paper's direct and continued violations of its permits. Our evidence showed over 1,000 individual violations of International Paper's air and water permits. They had built the mill for a particular capacity, had greatly increased that capacity over time, and in doing so had increased the pollution.

I explained that from my standpoint, I had nothing to lose. If I won the case for my clients, we could win big. If we lost, we had fought a good fight and had "worn the white hat." I took the position that neither I nor my clients would accept less than five million dollars.

Several meetings later, I received the call that IPC would pay the five million dollars total, if we could work out the many complicated details of settlement.

And complicated they were. We had to devise a fair way to divide the proceeds of the settlement among members of a class of lakefront-property owners in three different towns, with widely varying properties and property uses. Moreover, the class had been certified in 1980; now it was 1987, and in the interim many properties had changed hands through death, sales, subdivisions, and otherwise. Finally, as in many class actions, meaningful notice of the settlement had to be given to every class member, but only after approval by the presiding judge.

Ultimately, our original clients, the named plaintiffs in the action, acted as a "board of directors" on behalf of the class, and a complicated formula was agreed upon and approved for allocating the settlement fund among the now three hundred-plus class members. Aside from recovering for the class nuisance damages equaling approximately twenty-five percent of their properties' assessed value, the most exciting aspect of the settlement was the establishment of a $500,000 trust fund for research projects involving the environment of the south lake. The corpus of that trust now exceeds $750,000, and the trust has been awarding grants annually.

10. Good Cop, Bad Cop

For those toiling in the criminal justice vineyard, there is nothing more pleasing than good police work. On the other hand, there is nothing that is a greater threat to undermine the criminal justice system—in fact, society in general—than bad police work. Examples of both have brought people through the doors of the Addison County Courthouse.

The best and most courageous piece of police work that I ever ran across came out of an unsung incident and involved Walter Lamere, a sergeant in the Vermont State Police who was in charge of the Middlebury barracks. It culminated in the arrest of Arthur Gibeault.

Art owned a farm located on the north side of Route 125 about a mile west of Middlebury village. He was a successful dairy farmer and a successful trader in used farm machinery. Most of the time he was a lot of fun. He had a good sense of humor and was good company. He was also known to take a drink or two. At times, he could become pig-headed and, rather than behave in his usual easygoing way, he could become tough as nails.

One night, Art was out late, and after having had a few drinks, he decided to jack a deer. He was over in the Rochester area, and there he succeeded in jacklighting and shooting a deer at the back of a long, narrow mountain meadow. As Art was dressing his recent kill, along came a game warden who had been called to the scene by a neighbor who had heard the shot. The warden saw Art and started across the field. Art saw him coming and took off. Despite the darkness of the night, there ensued a chase through the woods. The circuitous path taken by Art reached a small cliff with about a fifteen-foot drop. That didn't bother Art at all—he jumped off the cliff, landing in such a way that he broke his left ankle. Even that did not stop him, and, broken ankle and all, he continued on through the woods until he had circled back to where he had left his pickup truck. He had succeeded in eluding the warden. Art got into his truck and somehow managed to drive himself approximately twenty-five miles to Porter Hospital, in Middlebury. There, they operated on his ankle and put him in a cast, which he lived with for the next several months.

As Art grew older, he got more cantankerous. His marriage deteriorated and he sometimes became downright ornery. As a longtime citizen, a prominent farmer, and as one who simply got around the county in his farm machinery dealings, he was known to all the police officers, including Walt Lamere. Walt had started his state-police career as a trooper in Middlebury in the 1950s and had returned as a sergeant to take charge of the Middlebury barracks.

One evening, the state police dispatcher got a call telling her that Art had barricaded himself in his barn, had several rifles and ammunition, and was threatening to kill anybody and everybody who approached him. The local police departments and the Vermont state police did not have any type of swat team, and thus those called to the scene were officers who were unaccustomed to this type of situation and untrained in methods for dealing with it. As the highest ranking state police officer in the county, Walt was called to the scene. By the time he arrived, various other police officers, with their cruisers' lights flashing, had taken up positions in anticipation of a possible shoot-out. Walt sensed that to allow this matter to continue in its present form was going to lead to a disaster. There was a real danger that his young officers could be injured or killed, and certainly that Art's life would be in jeopardy.

After sizing up the situation, Walt took it upon himself to take off his guns and to shout to Art that he was coming out to the barn to talk to him and that he didn't expect to be shot at. He then proceeded to walk from the area near Route 125 to the barn where Art was holed up. He became an easy target, and he fully recognized that he was risking his own life to try to prevent the possibility of a disastrous shoot-out. To everyone's relief, his strategy worked. He was able to reach the barn, and actually to sit down and talk to Art. A few minutes later, Art and Walt came out of the barn, unarmed, and got into Walt's cruiser, which headed for Porter Hospital. The criminal acts of Art Gibeault were finally resolved without a jail sentence, for his whole situation was treated as a mental-health problem triggered by the use of alcohol.

The entire episode took less than an hour and will not go down in history as any significant event. I hesitate to think, however, what would have happened had it not been for Walt's cool head and his willingness to take risks to protect others. In my mind it was the most unselfish and courageous piece of police work I ever ran into.

The worst cop scenario involved a man by the name of Paul Lawrence. Fortunately for Addison County, he was not here very long.

Paul broke into police work in the late 1960s, at the time when the use of marijuana and other drugs was becoming more popular throughout the country. His career was built on the anti-drug hysteria that followed this popularization. His career is documented in *Mocking Justice*, a book by Hamilton Davis. Paul started his career in 1966 as a Burlington police officer and then moved on to the state police. He soon became involved in an incident in Rutland, where he claimed he had been shot at. The windows of his police cruiser had, in fact, been shot out, but it appeared that the bullet had come from the inside of the cruiser rather than the outside. This event raised the eyebrows of a few people and made them wonder about his credibility. In any case, he moved on from the state police to the Brattleboro police department as an undercover agent. His credibility again came into question. A group of lawyers, including judges, came to the conclusion that he was not to be trusted. But somehow, his lack of credibility did not prevent him from being able to move on to another police department. His next stop was

Bennington, and that's where I ran into him personally for the first time.

In August of 1971, I was retained by a young man, Paul Kelly. He told me that from time to time he used marijuana but had never sold it. Nevertheless he had been arrested on the charge of a sale of marijuana to an undercover officer by the name of Paul Lawrence. Paul Kelly was a nice looking young man with long hair, and appeared to be a part of the anti-establishment culture that had grown up protesting the Vietnam war. The affidavits filed with the charge indicated that Paul Lawrence had purchased a small amount of marijuana from Kelly, and that the sale had taken place at a specific location in Bennington. My client admitted he had been near the location on the date alleged in the information and that he had had a conversation with Paul Lawrence, but there had been no mention of drugs and, certainly, no sale made to Paul Lawrence. The case became a swearing contest between a police officer, who produced a baggy containing some marijuana that he claimed to have purchased from my client, and the long-haired, anti-establishment young man.

It was hard to believe a police officer would make up a case out of whole cloth, but I was convinced my client was telling the truth. This was reinforced, not only by my client's candor, but by the fact that my investigation into the background of Paul Lawrence indicated that on several previous occasions there had been similar incidents where there was no evidence other than a one-on-one swearing contest. Some background-checking in Rutland and Brattleboro made it obvious that Lawrence's reputation for truth and honesty was not good in the legal community. I talked to Judge McClellan of Rutland and Judge Carnahan in Brattleboro, who both asserted that, under oath, they would testify that Paul Lawrence had a very bad reputation for truth and honesty. I decided to call the two judges as character witnesses and put into issue Lawrence's reputation for truthfulness. This would, I hoped, balance the word of a police officer swearing he bought drugs against the opposite testimony of a long-haired young man who would have to admit that he had used marijuana.

The case came on for trial in Bennington before Judge Hilton "Spike" Dier, Jr., and Judges McClellan and Carnahan were subpoenaed. When the time came for me to call them to the stand, they claimed they had a judicial privilege and couldn't be subpoenaed. I had never heard of such a privilege and asked the court to direct them to testify. Without the benefit of any precedent, Judge Dier granted the request of his two fellow judges, allowing them to escape taking the stand, under a doctrine of judicial privilege, newly created by himself—Judge Dier!

I then asked for a continuance so that I might get other members of the criminal-justice community to testify as to the reputation of Paul Lawrence for truth and veracity. My motion for a continuance was denied. The case went to jury and my client was convicted.

We appealed the case to the Vermont Supreme Court and in December, 1973, they handed down a decision[15] saying that I was right that there was, in this context, no such thing as judicial privilege. They did not, however, overturn the conviction, ruling that I had not been specific enough in defining the criminal-justice community as the relevant community for them to allow me to put Lawrence's reputation into contention. This was despite the fact that there were four pages of the trial record where I specifically laid out the background concerning what the judges would testify to and the type of testimony I could obtain if a continuance were granted.

My client went to jail for a crime he didn't commit. He was not alone.

After his stint in Bennington, Paul Lawrence came to Addison County as chief of police in Vergennes. John Deppman was our state's attorney, and after a very short time his suspicions about Lawrence were aroused. The Addison County bar has always been a small bar whose members, while contentious in court, have usually had a cordial relationship among themselves. There was a prevailing belief that fellow members of the bar could be trusted, and that they would not take unjust positions simply to gain advantage in a case. Deppman met with members of the bar who had had dealings with Lawrence, and, based upon those conversations and his own observations, he went to the Vergennes City Board of Aldermen and told them he would no longer prosecute any cases brought in by Lawrence unless there was independent verification of his story. This effectively ended Lawrence's tour in Addison County.

Lawrence then moved on to St. Albans. The district judge in Franklin County at that time was perhaps the most law-and-order judge in the state, Judge Carl Gregg. The town fathers there were concerned with what they saw as a growing drug problem, especially involving young people who hung around the park in the center of St. Albans. They bought into Paul Lawrence's pitch and hired him as an undercover police officer. Here, over the next several months, he claimed to have made dozens of one-on-one buys from young people who were the brought into court with only their testimony to stand against the sworn testimony of this police officer and the package of drugs he claimed to have bought from them.

One of them, a young man whom I had represented over the years, was Ronald Rich, who was accused of making a sale of heroin to Lawrence. The sale was supposed to have taken place at the rest stop on Route I-89, just south of St. Albans.

Ronnie, at fourteen, had been sent to the juvenile facilities at the Weeks School in Vergennes as a result of a petty theft. At age seventeen, without ever having been convicted of a crime, he had been transferred from the juvenile facility to the so-called house of correction, which was in reality a part of the state prison in Windsor, Vermont.

I had gotten into the Rich case a few days after the newspapers carried the story of a legislative inspection of the prison facilities at Windsor. Before they finished the tour, they were brought down to the death-chamber where the electric chair was still assembled, and, in the cell next to it, there was a young man, obviously still in his teens, naked, with nothing but a steel bunk to sit on. The legislators were astounded, and they went public with what they saw. The papers picked up on this and it proved to be an embarrassment for the prison authorities. Somehow Ron got my name and he asked me to come to the state prison to see him. He told me this story: After being sent from the Weeks School to what he'd been given to understand was the house of correction, he had complained that he was not being lodged in the house of correction, but in the wing of the facility which was actually the state prison. Apparently, he was rather adamant in his appeals, and as punishment, he was placed, naked, in solitary confinement next to the electric chair.

I went back to my office and prepared a writ of habeas corpus to order the authorities to show cause why he should continue to be incarcerated, claiming that his incarceration was unconstitutional. I filed it with the supreme court, which then had the trial jurisdiction for habeas-corpus petitions. Two days after filing the petition, I read in the morning paper that Ronald Rich had dismissed me as attorney and had withdrawn his petition. Not having been informed of this by Ron himself, I called him for an explanation, and he asked me if I would come down to the state prison as soon as possible. Within ten minutes I was in my car and on my way for the almost two-hour drive.

When I arrived there, he told me that on the night of the day I had filed the writ of habeas corpus, he had been awakened, taken out of his cell, and told, in the presence of the head of the parole board and the warden, that if he'd withdraw the petition, he would be released in a very short period of time. Ron refused the offer and was sent back to his cell. A short time later, he was taken out of his cell for another meeting with the officials. This time, they said that if he didn't withdraw this complaint, his father, who was on parole, would be accused of violating it and brought back to jail. His father had a long criminal record, and if his parole were violated he would be looking at a long stint in jail. Ron still wouldn't agree to dismissing me as his attorney and withdrawing the writ of habeas corpus. He went back to his cell. He was called out a third time and again presented with his alternatives—he could go forward with me as his attorney and with the writ of habeas corpus or he could withdraw the writ, fire me, and see that his father did not go to jail. This time, he agreed to follow the advice of the warden and the chairman of the parole board. They dictated two letters, which he wrote in his own hand—one to the supreme court calling for a withdrawal of the writ and another addressed to me dismissing me as his attorney.

While at Windsor that day, I reduced what he had told me to an affidavit. When I got back to the office, I had received in the mail the letter dismissing me. I immediately informed the supreme court that, in fact, the petition was not being withdrawn and that I was still acting as Rich's counsel. The supreme court set a hearing about the matter, to be held before the full court a few days later. I arrived in Montpelier early for it, and having some free time, wandered over to the state house, where the governor's office was then located. Phil Hoff, who was governor, happened to be in and I was able to tell him the background of the circumstances, as I understood them in the Rich case. I gave him a copy of Rich's affidavit and then left for the supreme court. I filed five copies of the affidavit with the clerk, who sent them into the court's chambers for perusal by the judges.

A short time later, Deputy Attorney General Chet Ketchum and I were asked to come into the chambers of the court. The court told me, informally, that while they thought the matters contained in the affidavit were serious, they did not believe the affidavit should be made public at this time and that I should withdraw it. I indicated that I would think about it, and Chet Ketchum and I left the chambers. A few minutes later, the court came into session. Chief Justice

Holden addressed me and said, "Mr. Langrock, is it your intention to withdraw the affidavit?" I responded, "Your Honor, as an officer of this court, I have filed the document and as far as I'm concerned, it is a matter of public record." Judge Holden said, "Mr. Langrock, I don't think you heard me. I think it is appropriate for you to withdraw this affidavit." I responded, "Perhaps, Mr. Chief Justice, you didn't hear me, but as an officer of this court, I have simply filed a document and the court may treat it as it wishes." At this point, Justice Holden's face became flushed and he turned to the clerk of the court, Norman Paduzzi, and said, "Mr. Paduzzi, would you please collect the affidavits and give them to Mr. Langrock." Norm Paduzzi, who was a good friend and rather mild-mannered, went down the row of judges sitting at the bench. He picked up each of their copies of the affidavit and then, at the chief's direction, handed them to me. At this point, the chief said "The court is adjourned."

To say the least, I was agitated. I turned on my heel with the five affidavits in one hand, my briefcase in the other, and started walking out of the courthouse. Norman caught up with me on the front steps of the courthouse and said, "Peter, don't do anything rash." I didn't—I simply put the affidavits in my briefcase and left for home. The case, however, had attracted the press, who were there for the hearing. I had decided that, discretion being the better part of valor, I would not agree to their request for a copy of the affidavit. The next day, the headlines read "Mysterious Affidavit Filed with Supreme Court." The question of the contents of the affidavit became moot days later when Philip Hoff, the governor, released it to the press, calling for an investigation into the operation of the parole board.

While these proceedings were going on, things were not quiet at the state prison. Ronnie had been moved from the holding cell in the death chamber back to his own cell. Here, his sleep was interrupted several times at night by guards banging on his door and shining lights in his eyes. The warden sought an administrative transfer from the state prison to the state hospital, claiming Ronnie had been placed without his clothes in the holding cell because he was suicidal. The transfer order had been signed by the governor without his recognizing its significance. On Thanksgiving Day weekend of 1967 the governor called me personally to apologize for signing the transfer order and said that he was immediately having Ronnie transferred back to the Weeks School. In less than a month, Ronnie was released from the Weeks School. The resulting political investigation brought about a complete upheaval and reorganization of the parole board and the personnel serving on it.

Juveniles in court proceedings were not guaranteed their constitutional rights at that time. In connection with the Rich case, I requested that this inequity be corrected. It was not, until much later, by action of the U.S. Supreme Court. However, the decision in the Rich case did hold that it was not permissible to transfer a child from inherently protective custody—a juvenile facility—to a correctional one.[16]

Later, I represented Ron on a charge of petty larceny and in a series of traffic violations.[17] During all of our relationship, he had never lied to me. With this background, I felt I knew Ronnie quite well, and when he told me he had made no sale of heroin to Paul Lawrence, I believed him. In spite of Ron's problems with the law, or possibly because of them, he was just not stupid enough to make a sale of heroin to an unknown person who could possibly have been an undercover agent.

I was faced with a problem of how to defend him. Once again, we had a police officer with a container of heroin and sworn testimony that he had bought it from Ronnie Rich. On the other hand, I had a young man who had been in trouble on many occasions, who simply claimed he had not sold it. I thought that if I could bring before a jury a number of other people who had also been unjustly accused, we might be able to undermine Lawrence's credibility and win the case. My frustration was that, knowing Judge Carl Gregg as I did, I doubted he would allow that type of testimony. This would mean first, a jury trial with a probable conviction, and then another trip to the supreme court. I lay awake many nights thinking about the best way to deal with this.

About this time, several defense attorneys, including Jim Levy; Joe Cahill, the public defender; and I, went to Attorney General Kim Cheney and told him of our concerns that in Paul Lawrence the state had a really bad apple. Kim Cheney assigned Assistant Attorney General Bill Keefe to do an investigation. Keefe's investigation was cursory and he exonerated Paul Lawrence, in spite of the fact we had been able to produce more than ten polygraph examinations of individuals who had been accused and who had denied their sales and had passed the lie detector tests.

It was a very frustrating time. There was a general knowledge within the law-enforcement community that young people were being ramrodded into convictions, sometimes even accepting plea bargains to ensure a lesser sentence, and many powers-that-be had grave suspicions about what was going on. Still, none of them seemed to have the strength of character to side with accused persons, even though they carried the presumption of innocence by law, in the face of a single lying police officer. There were two exceptions to this, Patrick Leahy, now our senior U.S. senator, and his deputy, Frank Murray.

Pat at that time was state's attorney of Chittenden County. He was engaged in a race for the United States Senate and, while concerned about any matters that would make him appear to be soft on crime, he could not tolerate the idea of a lying police officer putting innocent people in jail. He arranged for an undercover agent from New York, whose nickname was "the Rabbi," to come to Burlington. It was at this time that Paul Lawrence was on loan as an undercover agent to the Burlington police department. The Rabbi took a position in the park in front of city hall in Burlington, and four officers, at Leahy's direction, were placed near various buildings, keeping him under surveillance. After a short period of time, Paul Lawrence walked through the park. He never approached the person known as the Rabbi, but he went back to his office and filled out an affidavit saying he had made a purchase from him.

This was the beginning of the end of Paul Lawrence. Leahy started a prosecution against him. Governor Salmon appointed Robert Gensburg as a special prosecutor. Lawrence was eventually convicted of perjury and he went to jail. Leahy won his senate race.

Sometime later, when Tom Salmon was governor, he signed seventy-one pardons for people who had been convicted based upon the sole testimony of Paul Lawrence. I also ended up as lead counsel in fifty-five civil-rights cases against Paul Lawrence and some prosecutors, which resulted in a substantial, but still inadequate, settlement for those who were unjustly convicted. The tragedy is that at least in part because of Lawrence's false accusations some of Lawrence's victims committed suicide.

It is hard to look back at the eight years it took to break through the establishment's anti-drug hysteria to get to the simple truth. Such hysteria continues today.

Paul Lawrence was indicted in a federal court in New Jersey in November of 1996 on charges of forging records to mislead customers of his environmental firm about the disposal of six million pounds of contaminated soil. At least these charges didn't arise from corrupt police work.

11. Homicide Cases and the Tribulations of Defense Counsel

The Addison County Courthouse was filled with spectators carrying their brown-bag lunches when Charlotte Mahoney, charged with first degree murder in the shooting death of her husband, Howard, was tried. The Mahoneys had already had some domestic problems and were well enough known in their home county, Franklin, that the venue was changed to Addison.

Charlotte was a most interesting person. During World War II she was a passenger on a ship that was torpedoed and sank. She managed to get to a life boat and was rescued. The experience, however, had caused her hair to turn white. She was quite striking, in her mid-thirties, with a good figure, a pretty face, and that full head of snow white hair.

Charlotte was accused of having fired three bullets into her husband, killing him on the 6th day of May, 1961. The rifle, which she kept in her bedroom, had been given to her by her husband because she had told him she had seen a prowler. On the day of his death, Howard Mahoney had aroused Charlotte's temper by refusing to berate a neighbor over something inconsequential that Charlotte felt had been a slight to her. After shooting him, Charlotte took the empty cartridge cases, threw them into the furnace, and then calmly called the police and told them what she had done.

Bill Goldsbury of St. Albans was the state's attorney for Franklin County, and Tom Debevoise was attorney general. Together they made a presentation to the Franklin County grand jury, which indicted Charlotte Mahoney for first degree murder. At the time, this charge carried a sentence of death in the electric chair. Charlotte retained the services of Joseph Wool and his partner, Saul Agel, as defense counsel. Joe had defended Donald Demag, who in 1954 was the last person to have been executed in the state of Vermont.[18] Thankfully, he is still the last person to have been executed in the state.

In the late 1950s, Vermont adopted a new set of rules of procedure which followed the Federal Rules of Civil Procedure very closely. In a case prosecuted by Stella Hackel, who later ran unsuccessfully for governor of Vermont and was then appointed Treasurer of the United States, a defendant, Eldridge B. Williams, attempted to extend the discovery portion of these rules by trying to take a deposition in a criminal case. The Vermont Supreme Court responded on January 3, 1961, by handing down an opinion holding that the change in the rules of procedure did not apply to criminal cases.[19] The court said that to depart from the common law and permit defendants to have broad discovery powers would require much more specific legislation. The Vermont legislature for 1961 convened the day after the decision was handed down, and, under the guidance of then State Senator James Oakes, quickly passed a statute specifically extending to criminal cases a defendant's right to take depositions. This gave Vermont defense attorneys the broadest discovery procedures of any state in the country.

With the new statute in effect, Joseph Wool attempted to take the depositions of three of the police officers who had investigated the Mahoney homicide. The state objected, saying the legislature may have provided for the taking of witnesses' testimony, but only to "an occurrence witness who beholds or otherwise has personal knowledge of the crime" certainly not to a police officer.

The question of the scope of the new statute was of sufficient importance to be passed on to the Vermont Supreme Court before the trial took place. In an opinion filed on December 15, 1961, the court said, in effect, if the legislature is crazy enough to extend discovery into criminal cases, we'll let them stew in their own juices and not limit it in any way.[20] This decision marked the end of trial-by-ambush and the dawn of a new era of the right of the defendant to know what is happening in a criminal case. To this day, Vermont has the broadest provisions of discovery in the country, allowing defendants more information before trial than any other state.

By the time the Mahoney case came up for trial, in March of 1962, Tom Debevoise had resigned as attorney general—on January 2, 1962. He was replaced by Charles J. Adams of Waterbury (not the attorney Charles Adams of Middlebury). Adams ended up trying the case, which had been moved to the Addison County Courthouse pursuant to a motion for a change of venue.

Joe Wool had attempted to get permission from his client to enter an insanity defense. Charlotte refused, even in the face of a possible death sentence. At one point Joe appealed to her parish priest in desperation and said, "She's my client, but she's insane, and she won't listen to me." The priest then talked to Charlotte and suggested that she follow Joe's advice. Her response was to fire the priest and look for another confessor.

A couple of days before the trial, Charlotte was transported to the Addison County Courthouse to meet with her attorney so she could be acclimated to the surroundings and not have to see the courtroom for the first time when it was filled with potential jurors, spectators, and court officials. Joe pointed out to her where they would be sitting and she promptly sat down, crossing her legs. She inquired of Joe, "Which way do I look better, crossing my legs away from the jury or towards them?" Joe had his work cut out for him.

Joe had rented a house in Middlebury for the duration of the trial and enjoyed the celebrity-like status he was receiving from the newspapers and the spectators in the trial being followed by almost everyone in the state. In the course of the presentation of the evidence in the trial, Joe brought out every possible bit of evidence he could to justify Charlotte's shooting of her husband. His approach could be equated with a battered woman's defense in today's terminology.

When the jury retired to deliberate, Joe and entourage retired to the Pine Room in the basement of the Middlebury Inn. In 1962 this was Middlebury's prime watering hole. Generations of lawyers had waited there for jury verdicts. It was the same place where Jim Donaway, the most prominent lawyer in Middlebury during the 1920s and 1930s, ended his work days, using it as his office for meeting clients.

In due course the jury returned a verdict, and a call was made to the Middlebury Inn for defense counsel to return to the courthouse. The spectators filed in to hear the announcement of the verdict before a packed courtroom. Joe sat down at counsel table. Charlotte expressed no concern about what the verdict would be, and appeared concerned only about how she presented herself to the court at this dramatic moment. She looked at Joe, and smelling the results of the libations at the Pine Room on his breath, said, "You've been drinking!" and turned away from him, refusing to look back at any time until after the jury announced its verdict.

The verdict was not guilty of murder, but guilty of the lesser offense of manslaughter, and thus Charlotte had not only escaped the electric chair, but had in fact escaped a conviction of either first- or second-degree murder. The maximum sentence for manslaughter was fifteen years, and Charlotte was subsequently sentenced to serve twelve to fifteen years.

There was another chapter in this case when Bernard Leddy's Burlington firm represented Howard Mahoney's parents before the Supreme Court of Vermont. The probate court decreed the residue of Howard's estate, amounting to a total of about $3,000, to his mother and father instead of to Charlotte. Charlotte, this time representing herself, took the matter to the supreme court. The probate court's decision was reversed and sent back for a determination as to whether Charlotte had been guilty of voluntary or involuntary manslaughter, on which the financial outcome would depend. In a concurring opinion, Justice Percival L. Shangraw put this last chapter of the Mahoney case in perspective: "To continue this litigation, even though the parents should ultimately prevail, may well be, at least money-wise, like digging a hole to get the dirt to fill another hole."[21]

In 1968 Charles Barrett was arrested in St. Albans, in Franklin County, on a charge of first degree murder. The body of Clifton Combs had been discovered in the alleyway behind the police station, just west of Main Street. Combs had been stabbed in the eyes, his throat had been cut from ear to ear, and there were a total of more than fifty additional stab wounds—including sixteen in the heart, which, according to the pathologist, were administered after death.

The police were soon able to focus on Charles Barrett, and they approached him as to his possible involvement. He confessed and showed the police where a watch and wallet taken from the deceased had been hidden. This case arose before the creation of a Public Defender's system in Vermont, and a St. Albans lawyer, George Costes (later District Court Judge George Costes), was appointed as Barrett's attorney. George asked me to assist him in the trial of the case.

The two possible defenses we had were insanity and self-defense. Barrett had indicated that he and the deceased, Clifton Combs, had been drinking together and that he had been trying to help the deceased home, up a back alley behind the police station, when the deceased suddenly pulled a knife and attacked him. Barrett claimed he wrestled the knife away from Combs, cutting himself in the process. On seeing blood, Barrett said he went berserk and attacked Combs, resulting in the fifty-seven stab wounds, sixteen of which were administered posthumously to the heart.

The case was tried by jury. I will always remember my closing argument. It was probably the worst I had ever made. In trying to convince the jury of the insanity defense, I pointed out the incredible rage that must have invaded the mind of my client. "Just think of it, sixteen stab wounds in his heart after he was dead!" I then proceeded to hammer slowly on the rail with my fist—one, two, three, four, and as I looked up, the jury were all crossing their arms in front of their chests and sinking deeper into their seats. A thought came to my mind like a bubble in a cartoon strip: I pictured a coffin, my client's coffin, with sixteen nails in it, and I was hammering them shut. Having reached the number four, I was not in a position to stop counting. I had to proceed through my imitation of all sixteen stabs to the heart. Needless to say, the jury convicted my client of first-degree murder. There was no way they were going to let anybody with the potential for that type of rage go free.

It may or may not have been my worst closing argument, but it certainly made an impression on the jurors. Some years later, I was participating in a Community Players' production at the Middlebury Inn. We had a matinée performance that was attended by a large number of senior citizens. After the production, one of the audience came up to me and said, "Mr. Langrock, you don't remember me, but I sat on one of your juries once." I inquired as to what case had been involved, and she said, "I don't remember the name. It was a murder case, but you probably wouldn't remember it." I responded, "I remember every murder case I've ever tried." She then said, "Well, all I can really remember is that there were sixteen stab wounds to the heart." After a period of more than fifteen years, my driving home of those sixteen stab wounds into the heart had remained with her like nothing else in the case.

Fortunately, as it turned out for my client, Judge Sylvester refused to instruct the jury on the law of self-defense, saying he did not believe it was a self-defense case. On appeal, the Vermont Supreme Court reversed the ruling, pointing out that while "sixteen stab wounds in the chest do not necessarily suggest self-defense," the defendant was still entitled to have the jury make that determination.[22]

Just recently, while sitting in the dentist's chair, I was visiting with the dental assistant about the new courthouse. She recalled that in junior high school her social science teacher, Marshall Eddy, had taken their class to the court to watch a trial. Marshall was the top man in his class at Middlebury College and a honor graduate of the University of Michigan Law School. The trial to which he took his class was Barrett's retrial.

AN ASIDE

Marshall Eddy was the first lawyer in a family of doctors: his grandfather, Stanton Eddy, was a legendary country doctor who traveled around Middlebury in his horse and buggy during the early part of the century to deliver the new additions to the county population. One of the babies he delivered was Stanton "Stan" Lazarus, whose parents named their son after the good doctor. Stan ran the family department store on Main Street, and he served in the Vermont legislature in the late 1950s and early 1960s. He was one of the young turks who in 1962 helped Vermont elect Philip Hoff, the state's first Democratic governor in more than a century. In 1964, he served as executive clerk, the liaison between the legislature and the governor. Stan was a kind and generous man who personally fit virtually every local child's first pair of shoes in his department store. He also performed numerous local charities anonymously.

After graduating from law school, Marshall Eddy joined our firm. Given his local roots, his good brains, and his excellent education, we thought we had acquired a future star at the bar.

Our office was representing a young woman who had been present when her husband and his brother had shot and killed their father and the father's mistress in a remote cabin. They then fled the scene, leaving the dead couple's year-old baby in the cabin in sub-zero weather. The fact that the child froze to death exacerbated the crime. The young wife, our client, had at one point attempted to phone the authorities over the location of the child, but, frightened for her own safety, she didn't. The case later became the cover story for *True Detective* magazine. Marshall took on the principal responsibilities for the defense of this young woman. He finally worked out a plea to manslaughter, with a four-to-five year sentence that was based on her willingness to testify in the prosecution of her husband his brother.

Shortly thereafter Marshall came to see me. He told me that he wanted to spend his life trying to prevent the type of tragedy he had seen in the case rather than to pick up the pieces after it happened, and that he had applied for a position as a teacher at Middlebury Union High School. He got a teaching job in social science and soon moved to teach his true love, art. For years he has headed up the high school art department. Generations of students will attest to the great teacher Marshall is and how he has worked toward his goal of helping prevent problems. This was the teacher who took his class to the second trial of Charles Barrett, held in the Addison County Courthouse as a result of a change of venue from Franklin county.

At the *Barrett* retrial, the facts surrounding the killing were not the issue. The controversy centered around whether Mr. Barrett was temporarily insane or whether he had the intention to commit a premeditated murder. The psychiatrist for the defense, Dr. Cohen, described Mr. Barrett as a borderline personality who was mentally ill and, therefore, not responsible for his acts. The psychiatrist for the State was Dr. William Woodruff, a former Royal Air Force (R.A.F.) bomber pilot and a former London "bobby." Bill Woodruff was most cordial, with a quick mind. He loved nothing better than to be tested on cross-examination, and for years he was involved in most of the cases in Vermont where there were questions of insanity. At the first *Barrett* trial, he took control of the courtroom, while he was on the stand, explaining directly to the jury that my client was basically a sociopath—not mentally ill—and that he certainly should not be acquitted by reason of insanity. His direct testimony ended the next-to-last day of that trial.

Bill was all set to do a repeat performance during my cross-examination, scheduled for the following day. Thinking that discretion was the better part of valor, and not wanting to give him a chance to reiterate his effective testimony of the day before on the same day the case was going to be submitted to the jury, I, much to his chagrin, waived cross-examination. By the time of the second trial, I had changed tactics: hoping for a manslaughter rather than a murder conviction, I met with Bill before trial and he agreed to testify to the effect that, while my client was not insane and was a sociopath, he in fact did not have the requisite intent to commit a premeditated murder. The jury responded to this testimony by rejecting the state's plea for a first-degree murder conviction and, while not willing to go to the lesser charge of manslaughter, convicted Charles Barrett of second-degree murder.

After the jury verdict, my client was taken by the sheriffs to the back of the courtroom. I asked to be allowed to meet with him briefly in the room, which was on the second floor at the northwest corner of the courthouse. This was in the days before the requirement of shackles and handcuffs, and my client was allowed to visit me unadorned. I went into the room and I said, "Charlie, we have been through this before and we still have a chance on appeal." One might think that my client would have lost faith in his lawyer, having been convicted in the first trial of first-degree murder and now second-degree murder. To my surprise, he turned to me and said, "Peter, I have nothing against you. I think you did a good job, but that fucking jury...." At this point he took his fist and planted it forcefully in the middle of one of the three-by-four-foot panes of glass of the courthouse window. He hit it so hard that instead of the pane breaking, it merely jumped out in one piece from the molding, stood suspended in mid-air for a fraction of a second, and then crashed to the alleyway below. I backed towards the door and said, "Sheriff, I think he is ready to go now." My dentist's assistant's one specific recollection of the trial her class went to was the story of the window being broken.

On the appeal of the second case to the Vermont Supreme Court, I hired Marshall, now a teacher, to write the appellate brief on a contract basis. The stipend from the state for writing the brief went through our office directly to Marshall. Marshall and his wife, Jane, used these funds to pay the expenses of adopting a child, who rounded out their family of three biological children. Merritt Eddy an "All American Boy" of Native American, black, and Caucasian blood, grew up with my adopted son, Eric—also of mixed blood and a few years older—as a role model.

Marshall and Jane did as well with all of their children as he did with his students. Their daughter Serena represented the United States in the 1988 and 1992 Olympics in crew, a sport which caught her imagination when she was a student at Harvard.

This time, the Vermont Supreme Court affirmed Barrett's conviction.[23]

Some time later, the same window played a role in the history of the Addison County Courthouse. Steve Murray, who was on trial for attempted murder, made his appearance in court and then met with his counsel, Robert Keiner, in the very same room in the northwest corner of the second floor of the courthouse. It was wintertime, and there had been copious amounts of snow. The snow fell off the courthouse roof and formed a large snowbank along the northern edge of the building in the alleyway behind the courthouse and the Masonic hall. As Murray and Keiner completed their conference, the lawyer left the room with the expectation that the transporting sheriffs would enter the room and take Murray back to jail. His client had another idea: he grabbed the doorknob, pulled the door shut, and locked it from the inside.

While the officers were troubled by this development, they were not too disturbed, as there was only one door to the room. One of the sheriffs went in search of a key to open that door, while the other stood by it. Unbeknownst to the police, Murray opened the window, jumped from the second floor into the snowbank, and escaped. It wasn't until sometime the next summer that he was recaptured. Upon his recapture, he was arraigned not in the Addison County Courthouse but in Chittenden County, where he was also facing a kidnapping charge. There, State's Attorney Richard English asked for bail to be set at one million dollars. Then-Public Defender, now-Judge Michael Kupersmith, scoffed and said, "There is absolutely no reason for such ridiculously high bail." Judge Mandeville, who was sitting on the bench, listened intently, and then set bail at $750,000, which was believed to be the highest cash bail ever set in Vermont to that date.

In the early 1970s, the town of Bristol had a one-person police department: Police Chief Ceylon Dearborn. An occasion came when Ceylon was called to a domestic disturbance that had occurred in an apartment located south of the old movie theater (now a funeral home) on the road leading from Main Street down to the iron bridge and Lathrop's Mill. When he arrived, he found a fellow named Pierce in a rather agitated state. He talked to Pierce and tried to calm things down, but the altercation continued, with Pierce suddenly brandishing a broomstick and making threats at the chief. Ceylon placed Pierce under arrest, and, after a short scuffle, managed to handcuff him behind his back. He was marched up to the police cruiser but as Ceylon started to put him into the back seat, Pierce suddenly sprang away and started off in a dead run toward the embankment leading down to the river. Being handcuffed behind his back seemed to slow him down very little. Ceylon gave chase, hollered for him to stop, pulled his revolver from his pocket, and fired a warning shot in the air. Just as Pierce was reaching the steep embankment, he stopped, and Ceylon was able to catch him. There are two different accounts as to what ensued.

One thing for sure, Pierce was dead. His death was caused by a bullet from Dearborn's gun, the bullet having penetrated Pierce's right arm into his chest cavity and, finally, his heart.

The state police were called to investigate. Ceylon said the gun had fallen out of his holster, hit a rock, gone off and accidentally killed Pierce. This account was met with some skepticism by State's Attorney John Deppman. Deppman made the tough decision to bring a prosecution against Ceylon, one of the few town police officers in the county and a man with whom he worked on a regular basis. Ceylon was charged with manslaughter, and the case went to a jury trial. The State Attorney General's Office offered some help in the personage of an assistant attorney general named Bill Keefe.

Bill Keefe had a long career as an assistant attorney general and was known as a bulldog in homicide cases. When he retired a few years ago, he had been involved in prosecuting more homicide cases than any other lawyer in Vermont. We had crossed swords many times over the years and upon his retirement he gave his opinion of the three best defense lawyers in the state. Subsequently this sidebar appeared in *The Burlington Free Press*.

"Legal Laurels"

Middlebury lawyer Peter Langrock's draw as a criminal-defense attorney was increased twice in twenty-four hours recently.

When prosecutor William Keefe retired last month he named Langrock as one of the three best criminal-defense lawyers he had faced. Keefe had faced scores of lawyers while prosecuting suspects, including more than forty people charged with homicides.

The other two on the list were Barre lawyer Richard Davis and Burlington lawyer Charles Tetzlaff. Davis died July 26 after a battle with cancer, and Tetzlaff was confirmed that evening by the U.S. Senate to be the next U.S. Attorney for Vermont.

The Dearborn trial commenced in the Addison County Superior Court before Judge John Morrissey. In preparing for the defense of the case, I spent a lot of time with Ceylon trying to figure out what had actually happened. It was obvious the tale he had first told the police was factually inaccurate. There was no way that gun could have fallen from his holster, hit a rock and gone off accidentally, to send a bullet on the trajectory that killed Pierce. Unless we were able to come up with what actually happened, there was a strong chance of a conviction, and even after we pieced together the event, there was still the possibility of a conviction.

At our office we went through various scenarios of what might have happened by physically assuming the roles of Ceylon and Pierce and then acting out the chase and the altercation by the embankment. We finally concluded that when Ceylon had fired the warning shot into the air, he had not completed putting the revolver back into its holster. As Pierce approached the cliff area, he stopped in his flight and Ceylon grabbed Pierce's right arm with his left hand. The revolver was still in Ceylon's right hand. Pierce, lurching and trying to pull away, caused Ceylon to tighten his left-hand grip on Piece's arm. As a natural reaction, he squeezed both of his hands at the same time. The simultaneous squeezing of his right hand caused the gun to discharge. After the shot was fired, Ceylon dropped the gun, which was found next to a rock close to where Pierce had fallen. It was this rock Ceylon originally blamed as the cause of the gun having accidentally fired.

The facts were pretty straightforward at the trial. Ceylon testified quite effectively as to what actually must have happened. The state played heavily on the inconsistency of his first story, and suggested that a verdict of guilty was therefore appropriate.

In closing argument, I decided to present the jury with a reenactment. I took the gun that was in evidence, fired a theoretical warning shot in the air, grabbed an imaginary Pierce by the arm, squeezed his right arm with my left hand, and at the same time squeezed my right hand on the trigger and dry-fired the unloaded gun. As I heard the click of the firing pin, a flash went through my mind: "I'm going to have to drop the gun on the courtroom floor. If it falls to the left, my client will be convicted. If it falls to the right, as it had when found next to the rock, he will be acquitted. I can't not drop the gun."

I did drop the gun and, as it hit the courtroom floor, it seemed to almost teeter before it fell to the right and I could point to it and say, "and that's where the police found the gun." The jury acquitted, but I've always wondered what would have happened if the gun had fallen in the other direction.

After the case, Ceylon stayed on as Bristol's Chief of Police, and my fees were paid out of Federal Revenue Sharing Funds approved by a town vote.

In a subsequent case, Ceylon's investigating activities reached a high. Someone had shot an arrow into the face of the clock on the Bristol Town Hall, stopping the minute hand from moving. In interviewing a suspect, Ceylon remarked that it must have taken several arrows before he hit the face of the clock. The suspect was incensed and said, "It damn well didn't. I hit it on the first shot." Restitution for fixing the clock took care of the malicious mischief charge.

12. Changing Sexual Mores

Dealing with acts of violence against women is one area of the criminal law that has shown a major change in attitudes over the years. One evening in 1963 I received a call from the Middlebury police saying there had been a report of rape. I responded by going to the scene, which was a house occupied by a Middlebury College student, his wife, and their newborn baby.

The young wife, the alleged victim, recounted the story of what had happened. It appeared her husband was out at the library studying and she was home alone in the early evening with the six-month-old baby. A neighbor, a sergeant in the United States Army who was on the ROTC faculty at Middlebury College, knocked on her door. When she answered it, he asked if he could use her phone. She agreed, somewhat reluctantly, and he came into the kitchen. Instead of going for the phone, he reached for her, placed one hand in her crotch, and threw her against the refrigerator. She smelled alcohol on his breath and was frightened, not only for herself but for her baby. Just the day before, she had finished reading an article in the *Saturday Evening Post* about an ROTC officer at a midwestern college who had raped a young woman and then had killed both her and her baby.

The sergeant forcibly pushed her past the baby in the livingroom and up the stairs toward the bedroom. As he fell on top of her while pushing her up the stairs, she realized that her best chance of survival was to give in without a physical struggle. When they got to the bedroom, she asked him, in hope of gaining some time, if he had locked the front door. He said "No," and went down to lock the door. She knew her husband had a loaded .38 revolver in the bedside-table drawer. She opened the drawer, pulled out the gun, and realized that she was unsure how to use it. Afraid that a bluff with the gun might escalate the violence, she put it back. The sergeant returned to the bedroom, and he told her to undress, which she did. He undressed and then placed her hand on his penis, pushed her back on the bed, and had intercourse with her. Without saying another word, he dressed and left.

The woman was terrified, believing that he was coming back to shoot her and the child. She had locked all the doors and was crawling around on the floor in the kitchen so he would not be able to see her through the windows. She reached up to the counter and brought the phone to the floor, from where she called her husband, who finally answered the page at the library. The husband hurried home, she told him what had happened, and he called the police. In talking to her that night, I was certain that the fear she expressed was real and that her rendition was the truth.

An "Information," the charging document, was filed, and an arrest warrant was issued. The procedure was simply for the state's attorney to complete the document, sign it, and turn it over to a police officer to make an arrest.

The sergeant was arrested and taken to jail. At the arraignment the next day, he pled "not guilty" through his attorney, Jack Conley. He was released on bail, and the case was set on the trial calendar.

It came to light through the investigation that the same individual had been teaching women how to fire rifles at the ROTC facilities on campus. On at least one occasion at the firing range, he had grabbed a woman by the breasts when she was in the prone firing position. Although a complaint had been made to the college, no disciplinary action had been taken. It was made known to me the college wanted the rape charges to be turned over to the military authorities so the case could be handled without the publicity of a criminal trial. I was upset by the college's lack of candor with regard to the previous complaint about the activities at the firing range. No one at the college came forward with that information; I found out about it by way of the grapevine. I had a meeting with the college deans and told them I would look upon any future lack of cooperation on their part as an obstruction of justice. I declined their suggestion to turn the matter over to the military authorities. It was obvious the college personnel was worried more about the reputation of the college than they were about what happened to this young woman. Despite their motives, their suggestion may have been right, as we found out when we went forward on the rape charge to a trial before a jury.

The defense in the case was consent. At that time, when consent was an issue, a woman's previous sexual past was admissible, supposed to show that if she had loose morals at other times, she probably consented in the case in question. It turned out the alleged victim and her husband had been lovers before they married, and that in fact their child had been conceived before marriage. While this was not unusual in Vermont at the time, it was a factor the defense could play up to show how this young lady was a person of supposedly loose moral character.

The time for the trial came, and the victim testified. She was very bright and attractive, about nineteen years old. Her clothes were tight, probably from a slight gain of weight during her pregnancy, accenting her very real voluptuousness. In the course of her examination she was able to maintain her composure, but at each court recess she would break down in tears. Somehow, she would regain her composure before the jury came back, and would continue her testimony through some very difficult cross-examination without breaking down in front of the jury. Conley asked her questions as to why she did not yell out the window for help if she was in fact being raped, why she undressed herself, and why she actually placed her hand on the defendant's penis. She explained her belief that it was in the interest of her safety and that of her child to feign a consent rather than to vigorously and physically defend herself. In the course of the trial, it came out that as a method of birth control she and her husband were using *coitus interruptus*, with her husband withdrawing before he ejaculated. She testified that the sergeant ejaculated during penetration, causing the additional concern of a possible pregnancy. Thankfully, by the time of trial it was known she was not pregnant as a result of the sexual attack.

In his closing argument, Conley suggested that any normal, healthy, full-blooded woman would have resisted the attack, if in fact it was an attack, with all her strength. As a prop he used a needle, which he moved with one hand so as to miss contact with a piece of thread in his other hand. He suggested to the jury that it was very difficult to thread a needle or make a sexual entry if the intended recipient was moving in resistance. He then attacked her chastity and took the position that his client could not possibly know that in fact, under all the circumstances, she hadn't consented.

The jury retired and were in deliberations for only about twenty minutes before they brought back a verdict of not guilty.

I went down to my office on the first floor of the courthouse. I was devastated. I felt that there had been a total miscarriage of justice, and I didn't really know how to deal with it. As I was sitting there, Joe Wool, the dean of the defense bar in the state, opened my door and said to me, "Peter, it's about time you learn how to lose." I think I could have killed him on the spot. Fortunately, he shut the door quickly and was gone before I could reply. As time went on, I contemplated his comments and it made me realize that as an attorney, as a prosecutor for the state, I had to remain objective, and that losing was part of what I would have to deal with if I were going to be willing to try hard cases. The case taught me how difficult it was to convince a jury of a factual scenario that went beyond what they would commonly encounter in their lives. This young woman had intelligently made a decision not to meet violence with violence, out of fear for herself and her child. It was a good decision for her at that time and would be a good decision today. That jury in the early 1960s was unable to fathom that a young woman could make such a decision consciously. Then, reasonable doubt crept in, created by the position taken by the defense. How could the defendant have known his intentions were unwanted when she did not act in a fashion consistent with what almost every other "full-blooded American woman" would do?

If that case were tried today, none of the woman's premarital sexual relationship with her husband would have been admitted, and any attacks on her chastity and moral character would have been entirely excluded from evidence. No doubt today the same presentation of those facts before the same panel would result in a very short deliberation, but now the verdict would be guilty.

The case, which took place prior to the advent of courtroom television, caused an instant sensation in the local press. Each hearing was covered not only by the local *Addison County Independent*, but by *The Burlington Free Press* and the *Rutland Herald*. When the matter came to trial, the courtroom's back benches were crowded with observers. The acquittal made the front-page headlines of *The Burlington Free Press*, and in effect the rape victim became a victim for a second time.

Adultery or Racial Bias?

Nowhere are the changing sexual mores more evident than in connection with the way certain sexual activities are treated under the criminal law. In 1960 adultery was a felony in Vermont, punishable by up to five years in prison. Adultery remained a felony until the law was finally repealed by the state legislature in 1981. While it was not a crime into which a prosecutor initiated investigations, occasionally the facts were such that the legislatively defined crime could not be ignored.

In one instance, in the fall of 1961, I received a call from an irate wife. She told me her husband was at deer camp and was having an affair with a woman who was at the camp with him. I suggested she come around in the morning and we could talk about it then. She countered with, "You're the state's attorney, aren't you? Isn't adultery a crime? The evidence will be gone by morning!" As I knew both this woman and her husband and really did not think there was anything to be gained by initiating a criminal investigation, I stonewalled her, saying I would look into it on the morrow and that I just didn't have any police officer available to initiate an investigation that night. By the next day the call for a criminal investigation had cooled down.

In 1966 my only partner, Mark Sperry, and I were called upon to assist in the defense of a black minister who had been the object of some racial violence, including a shotgun being fired into his house. A state police officer who was supposedly assigned to protect him at his home came into the house to use the bathroom and claimed to have found him in a compromising position with a white woman. The minister was charged with adultery. While pursuing an equal-protection defense that this was a racially motivated prosecution, we researched the extent to which adultery was still being prosecuted. We found that over the previous decade there had been eighty-five convictions for adultery throughout all of the counties of Vermont, and that a large number of the defendants had actually gone to jail. It appeared that the usual scenario calling for jail was when a man left his wife to live with another woman and fathered children with her, causing an increased need to her and the children for public assistance. The adultery statute was used as a way of breaking up this relationship and was a rather harsh approach to what was essentially a welfare problem. Fortunately, in the case involving the black minister, the woman involved moved to California and refused to return to testify. The California courts refused to extradite her as a witness and the case was dismissed.

Proof of adultery required proof of actual intercourse and this was sometimes difficult to establish. Since 1778, when it was still an independent republic, Vermont had a statute on its books called the Blanket Act. That statute provided as follows:

Persons found in bed together

A man with another man's wife, or a woman with another woman's husband, found in bed together, under circumstances affording presumption of an illicit intention, shall each be imprisoned not more than three years or fined not more than $1,000.00.

The form of the indictment or information gives insight not only to the form of court pleadings, but to the intrinsic societal values that it incorporated.

Accusation of a man under the statute.

[He] then and there being [a married man, having a lawful wife then and there living, to wit, one ———,] was found in bed, together with one ——— (state the particular circumstances of such being found, so that the presumption of intent may appear); and the circumstances aforesaid then and there afforded presumption of an illicit intention, by and between him the said ———, and her, the said ———, then and there to have unlawful sexual connection with each other; she, the said ———, then and there not being [a married woman, and then and there being the wife of one ———, of ———, who then and there was still living].

How the legislature in its wisdom decided a five-year penalty was appropriate for those convicted of adultery, with only a three-year penalty for those who were convicted under the so-called Blanket Act, is still unexplained. The repeal of the Blanket Act preceded the repeal of the adultery statute by only two years.

Not surprisingly, society's attitude toward the use of sexually oriented language in public in the 1960s was substantially less tolerant than it is today. In one such case, in 1968, a young man had been at the New Haven Drive-In Theater and had gone to the refreshment counter to buy a box of popcorn. Standing in line, he pulled out a box of popcorn and said to the manager, "Is this what you mean by a large box?" The manager was apparently on a short fuse that night: he said he didn't like wise guys and that he wanted him to leave. My client told me that as he was walking out of the refreshment center, he looked back at the manager and called him a "fucking asshole." The next thing he knew, he had received a citation to appear before the Addison District Court to answer to a charge of using obscene language in public.

I went with him to the courthouse for the arraignment and we received a copy of the Information, which was signed by State's Attorney Ezra Dike. The document claimed that my client had used obscene language in public, but it did not make any specific references. Subsequent to receiving the Information, I filed a motion asking the State to specify exactly what it was that my client was supposed to have said. Judge Hilton "Spike" Dier denied my motion. At the jury drawing Ezra Dike got up and explained to the jury that the charge was one of using obscene language in public and asked the jurors if they thought they could render a decision based upon the facts in the case without ever making any specific reference to the words my client was supposed to have uttered. As they all indicated they would follow the law, he sat down.

It was then my opportunity to examine the jury to see if they would be fair and impartial. I started, "My client is accused of using two words that are supposed obscene. The first of these is the word asshole. Now, does that word offend any of you people sitting on the jury?" The courtroom was exceedingly quiet and the jury looked nervous, but no one responded positively to my inquiry. I continued, "The other word my client is accused of using is a derivative of a word we find quite commonly in literature today, a derivative of the word 'fuck,' or the word 'fucking.' In other words, my client is charged with calling the manager of the New Haven Drive-In a 'fucking asshole.' Now, does that offend any of you?" At this point, two young men in the back of the jury could barely contain themselves. They put their hands over their mouths and their bodies shook with laughter.

We finished the jury draw and that was the last I ever heard of the case. It was never called up for an actual trial, I never received word of a dismissal, and for all I know, it may still be pending. I can only suppose that the absurdity of using the criminal law to police language of that nature dawned on the powers that be and in one way or another the case was shuffled under the rug.

On the other hand, some transgressions were treated in the 1960s with a lighter hand than they might be today.

On one occasion, I was prosecuting an individual for bigamy. The evidence we had was a complaint from his third wife that he had been married twice before and had never obtained a divorce for either union. I obtained proof of the fact of the marriages and filed the charge of bigamy in the then-municipal court. The individual involved was represented by Joe Wool. I thought it was an open-and-shut case until Joe told me his defense. He said, "Peter, my client may never have gotten a divorce, but at the time he married his second wife, he was out of state, and as he was already married when that second marriage occurred, the second marriage was void." He then continued, "Before marrying his third wife, his first wife had passed on. Thus, as the first marriage had terminated in death, and the second marriage was void and occurred outside of your jurisdiction, he was perfectly free to marry the third person, and you have no basis for a prosecution." He was right, and I dismissed the charge.

On another occasion, a man had been imbibing quite heavily at the VFW. When the bar closed, he walked home. He apparently became confused and instead of entering his apartment, he entered the apartment next door. He went into the bedroom, took the cigarettes out of his shirt pocket and laid them on the night table, took off his shoes, shirt, and pants, and crawled into bed. As a way of saying goodnight to his wife, he reached behind him and grabbed her buttocks. Unfortunately for him, it turned out that the buttocks he grabbed belonged to the woman who lived in that apartment, not to his wife. The neighbor was quite upset, understandably, and called the police. He was arrested and brought to court the following Monday. By that time, the victim, while still angry, appreciated the humor of the situation. He was allowed to go free and sentenced only to time served, with a stern lecture from the court on his need to deal with his alcohol problem.

The Pearl Buck Will

Besides the adultery statute and the so-called Blanket Act, Vermont had on its books until 1977 a prohibition against fellatio.

"§2603: Fellation: A person participating in the act of copulating the mouth of one person with the sexual organ of another shall be imprisoned not less than one year nor more than five years."

On its face it prohibited any type of oral sexual contact even between spouses in the privacy of their bedroom. However, it was generally considered as a prohibition of homosexual activities. In the early 1970s most homosexual relationships were frowned upon and thought by many to be criminal in nature. Certainly no one ever considered the possibility of a marriage between two persons of the same sex.

It was in this context that the battle over the estate of the Nobel laureate Pearl S. Buck was set.

One of Pearl Buck's children, Edgar Walsh, called me in Middlebury and told this story. A few years earlier his mother had contacted an Arthur Murray Dance Studio in the hope of taking some dancing lessons. A young man by the name of Theodore Harris became her dancing teacher. Over a period of time, he came to her home and ingratiated himself with her. She appointed him her private secretary and he became her almost constant companion. My client was concerned that Harris was taking advantage of Pearl Buck's age and emotional vulnerability, and was garnering all her assets for his own benefit at her expense and, eventually, the expense of her one biological child and seven adopted children. I told my client there was really little that could be done. A very short period of time after that discussion, Pearl Buck, who had been quite ill, died. A will was offered for probate in the Rutland County Probate Court. It provided that a small amount of the royalties from the foreign rights to her work go to her children, with the rest of the estate, including her domestic royalties, going to Theodore Harris. An investigation of the facts showed that even those international royalties which the will had set aside for her children were no longer in her estate. Theodore Harris had had title to them transferred to his name prior to her death. This effectively meant her entire estate went to him, her dancing instructor.

The document offered to the court had been correctly signed and witnessed and was approved. On behalf of the children, Mr. Walsh asked me to file an appeal from the probate court to the Rutland Superior Court where we could have a jury determination as to whether the document that had been filed with probate was actually the true will of Pearl S. Buck, or whether it was the result of the undue influence of Theodore Harris.

The case came to trial before Hon. Franklin S. Billings, who was later chief justice of the Vermont Supreme Court, and, still later, chief federal district judge for the district of Vermont. A twelve-person jury was assembled with members from all over Rutland County.

During the pre-trial investigation, we learned that Theodore Harris was a homosexual, and we explored this issue to see what role it may have played in the determination by Pearl Buck of the object of her bounty. Fred Pope, the attorney on the other side of the case, representing Mr. and Mrs. Drake, friends of Harris who were the executors named in the will, accused us of gay bashing and thought our activities were reprehensible.

Whether it was gay bashing or not, Harris's sexual orientation became known to the jury during the course of the trial. We called a witness to the stand who was a friend of Theodore Harris. When he walked past the jury to the witness box, in an obviously effeminate manner, the courtroom, including the spectators and the press, became quite attentive. My partner, Fred Parker, did the direct examination. A most damning piece of evidence against Harris was that, according to this witness, one night after he and Harris had been drinking and began to feel chummy, Harris had said to him, "Throw in with me and when I get her under my control, you can share in her money." One could almost feel the cold shudder that rippled through the courtroom. The witness declined Harris's offer and went to bed. Further testimony that shortly afterwards Harris pursued him into the bedroom and attempted to have sex with him did little to help Harris's credibility.

I did the closing argument, and I asked the good Vermont jury to judge this case by the same standards by which the Nobel laureate, Pearl Buck, would have judged it herself. The jury was not out very long before they came back and announced their verdict.

Indeed, they had decided the will was the product of undue influence and not of the free will of Pearl Buck.

The children were now in control over the administration of the estate. Much to their dismay, they found there was very little left, as almost all of the copyrights and other assets of value had been transferred during her lifetime either directly to Harris or to a foundation that he controlled. Our job was now to get the assets back from him. The estate brought a lawsuit directly against Harris, and as the record of royalties due and received was quite traceable, it was virtually impossible for him to hide the assets he had obtained from Ms. Buck. Eventually a settlement was reached where 87 1/2 percent of the future royalties were returned for the benefit of the children.

An interesting aside to the case is that the Drakes took an appeal from the jury verdict to the Vermont Supreme Court. We considered moving to dismiss the appeal, based upon the fact that the Drakes, in their capacity as named co-executors, had no standing to take such an appeal. We rejected that approach as we thought it somewhat specious and that there should be a hearing on the merits of the case itself. Much to the Drakes' chagrin and our surprise, the court ruled that there was no proper appeal before them because the Drakes had no standing to take such an appeal. It is the only time I can remember ever winning an appeal on a theory we had rejected out of hand and had not even bothered to brief.

13. Unwinding Marriages

Divorce cases are always very serious happenings for the parties. Attorneys must remove themselves from the emotions involved and develop a sense of perspective, and sometimes a sense of humor, or they can be of no use to their clients. If they don't, they will not survive emotionally for very long and, as many have done, they may leave the field of family law altogether.

I am fired by about one of every ten clients seeking a divorce, but rarely by clients in other sorts of cases. I am often requested to take over from another lawyer in the middle of divorce proceedings—again, much more frequently than in the overall caseload.

In the divorce case, there are overlays of emotion arising out of the breakup of the marriage. These emotions range from anger to deep guilt. Clients feel rejected, hurt, and inadequate, and for a period of time they are on an emotional roller coaster calling more for the lawyer's skills as a counselor and advisor than as a legal scholar. This is compounded by the very real frustration a client feels in finding that the court will not necessarily award him or her the relief they feel is appropriate. On top of all this, the system often will not work on a timetable that accommodates clients' preconceived needs. The result is that the lawyer is often the scapegoat. In most cases, however, good lawyers can bring about positive results or, at least, make the best of a bad situation.

I recall quite vividly my representation of a lovely, gentle young woman who had fallen in love with and married a young man who subsequently came down with multiple sclerosis. As his physical condition deteriorated, so did his mental attitude, and the marriage declined to a point where she felt she had to leave. She was a teacher by profession and the daughter of a well-respected local family. My client wanted nothing from the rather meager marital estate; she simply wanted to live free of a steadily degenerating, unacceptable emotional situation.

One morning at home I received a phone call. It was her husband calling. "Mr. Langrock, I want you to know I have a revolver and three bullets. One is for my wife, one is for her father, and one is for you." This was not my idea of a pleasant breakfast conversation. I talked to him on the phone for an hour trying to get him to calm down and put what was happening to him in perspective. I had some success in improving the situation. Still, given his deteriorating condition, he considered himself as having little to lose, and I was concerned that he might really carry out his threat.

I concluded that nothing was to be gained by charging him as a criminal on account of his making the threat. His wife, my client, already had a significant emotional burden because of leaving him, and having him labeled a criminal or put in jail would only make it worse for her.

The man was distraught, not only because of the emotional upheaval of the divorce itself, but also because of his disease. I had, of course, informed my client of her husband's threat, and she told her father. We felt relatively safe, in the belief that nothing would happen before the court date.

This case took place in the mid-1960s when there was nothing comparable to our current court security measures. When the time came for the final hearing, I asked for a qualified deputy sheriff to be present in addition to the usual court bailiff. He stationed himself near the husband to make sure that nothing serious would happen, and it didn't. The case proceeded in a normal fashion. My client got a divorce and both parties went on their separate ways. I do not know what eventually happened to him, but my client met a young widower, remarried, and has lived happily ever since.

Prior to 1971 Vermont did not have a no-fault divorce provision. In order to obtain a divorce, the plaintiff—or the libelant, as the plaintiff was then called—had to prove that the libelee (the defendant) was at fault on one of several grounds. The grounds included adultery, desertion, and—the most popular charge—intolerable severity. To prove intolerable severity it was necessary to prove that the libelee had engaged in unacceptable physical or mental conduct against the spouse and that this conduct had adversely affected the health of the spouse. The degree of proof which was required to meet this standard varied tremendously from judge to judge. All divorces were then handled in the county courts, and as all the superior judges rode circuit throughout the entire state, there was not a single generalized standard that you could count on. Some judges were known to be tough, and in thin cases continuances were often requested until a more lenient judge rolled around in the rotation.

One of the judges toughest on a divorce was Harold "Hack" Sylvester. For the most part, when the other party did not contest the divorce, it took only a small amount of evidence to meet the necessary standard. In Judge Sylvester's courtroom, however, you could not count on obtaining a divorce in a close case, even if the matter was uncontested. I recall having lost five uncontested divorces, and they were all before Judge Sylvester.

On one particular occasion, I had a client who wanted a divorce, and we brought a suit claiming intolerable severity. The story she told me would have been sufficient for the granting of a divorce by virtually any judge but Judge Sylvester. Her husband did not want the divorce, and yet he did not really decide to contest it. At the time of the hearing, he appeared in court *pro se*, representing himself. We contemplated continuing the case until a more lenient judge was available, but my client was anxious to have the matter heard and over with. There was no evidence of actual physical abuse on the part of the defendant. We went forward on the idea that many things he had done had been intentionally destructive and, though verbal rather than physical in nature, were done deliberately to upset my client. We further offered testimony that this upset was significant and that it had affected her health, leaving her in a nervous and shaken state. The defendant sat motionless in court. He did not contest the allegations, but he made it clear to the court that he was not going to cooperate in any way with his wife getting a divorce. After presenting the case, the judge announced quite clearly that we had not carried our burden of proof and the parties would have to stay married.

As we walked back to the office, my client was obviously very distressed. She turned to me and said, "I know I should have told you." In response to the blank look on my face, she related that, shortly after she was married, she had come home and found her husband in bed with a young boy in a compromising situation. Had I known that, and with her consent had been able to present those facts to Judge Sylvester, I would not only have been able to get her a divorce, but would have had the option of obtaining all of the property of the marriage, as well as permanent and punitive alimony. We were barred from bringing a new action until there were additional acts of intolerable severity that occurred after the hearing.

Another divorce that Hack Sylvester heard was one involving the owner of a small independent telephone company. This man's wife was represented by Joe Wool, probably the best-known lawyer in Vermont at that time. I was not present in that hearing and became involved only when I later represented a woman who subsequently married the telephone-company owner.

At that time there was a statutory provision requiring divorce decrees to include a prohibition so that the defendant could not remarry for a period of two years after the granting of the divorce. The court had the power to waive the provision and this was often done where there was a woman in the case who was pregnant. Apparently the courts felt that the legitimizing of a child's birth was more important than punishing the defendant in a divorce case for the fault that was the basis for the divorce.

In this particular case, Judge Sylvester took a dislike to the husband and granted the divorce to the wife. He ordered a properly distribution giving everything to the wife, with the exception of the husband's stock in the telephone company. He then added on a substantial alimony provision. Ordinarily, the lawyers would prepare the final judgment order based upon the court's findings. In this case, Judge Sylvester's unfavorable view of the husband was so extreme he wasn't going to wait for the lawyers to prepare the order, and he prepared the judgment order himself. In decreeing the independent telephone company's stock to the husband, he apparently thought it was of little value, but that it represented the job from which the husband could earn the substantial alimony payments the judge also included in the order. However, in preparing the decree, and most assuredly as an oversight, he did not include the usual two-year prohibition against remarriage.

Shortly after the decree became final, and within the year, my client married the ex-husband. Thus, we had a marriage that ordinarily would have been prohibited but for the fact of Judge Sylvester failing to include the usual prohibitory clause in his order.

Within a few months after this second marriage, the man sold his stock in the independent telephone company to Continental Telephone & Telegraph for a sum in the millions. He and his new bride took off for a grand world-wide tour.

However, shortly after their return, he dropped dead. They had purchased some real estate jointly, with survivor's rights which, under the law, can exist only between a husband and wife. Because of this, and also because of her statutory rights as a wife, it appeared that everything of substantial value would be going to her. His death resulted, again by law, in the cessation of all alimony payments. His first wife and children were enraged over the fact that wife number one would get nothing whatsoever and wife number two would receive virtually everything. Even the children would get little or nothing from the estate.

Joe Wool continued to represent the first wife and children. I represented the second wife. Don Ferland of the firm of Conley & Foote, who later became a superior judge, represented the estate. Joe undertook an action to declare the second marriage void as having been solemnized during the period in which remarriage was prohibited by the statute. If he won, that prohibition not having been included in this final decree, the second marriage would have been declared void and the children would have been in a position to receive substantial assets. Our research indicated that we had a very strong case, but not without some risk. Joe was interested in trying to settle, but first we had to ascertain the nature and extent of the estate itself. In his whirlwind world-wide trip, the deceased had established bank accounts in four different countries and had purchased extensive property in Yarmouth, Nova Scotia. The time came for all of us to try to figure out what had actually happened in Nova Scotia, and Attorneys Wool, Ferland, and I journeyed there together.

Don Ferland had retained the services of Irving Pink, a leader of the Nova Scotia bar and quite prominent as a director of the Canadian Broadcasting Corporation. We arrived in Nova Scotia and met with Mr. Pink and representatives of the trust company that managed both the real property and the estate bank accounts. A young trust officer was assigned the responsibilities of making us feel at home in Yarmouth. After our meeting, we made reservations for dinner at what we believed to be Yarmouth's finest seafood restaurant.

The four of us arrived, and after a couple of martinis we proceeded to order the best on the menu—three-pound lobsters. As we placed the order, the face of the young trust officer paled. I am sure he was thinking to himself how could he ever possibly justify to his superiors a dinner as expensive as this one was going to be. His income was certainly not enough to pay for it out of his own pocket. Recognizing the symptoms immediately, I said, "Oh, by the way, this dinner is on us." At this point a look of relief passed over his face, and he too decided to have the three-pound lobster. Some time after our return to Vermont, the parties agreed to terms of a settlement that balanced the risks to either side and was fair both to the second wife and to the children.

In another divorce case, the husband's lawyer attempted to explain to his client, on the steps of the Addison County Courthouse, how the two-year prohibitory period worked. The lawyer was aware this man had a relationship with a woman, and he presumed they wanted to get married. He explained to his client that unless the court made an entry changing the length of the prohibitory time, he would not be able to marry this woman for a two-year period. The client listened attentively, and then, in all seriousness, turned to his lawyer and said, "Do you think you could get the judge to make it a five-year period?"

There was one more provision of the law in force during the 1960s that made the practice of divorce law a bit sticky. It was the doctrine of recrimination. This meant the plaintiff had to prove as a part of his or her case that he or she had been a good and faithful spouse. If both parties had had adulterous relationships, the law required they were doomed to stay married to each other forever. This law did not deal with the reality of the changing sexual mores. In many divorce cases the lawyer made only a cursory investigation into the question of the plaintiff's fault, and then at trial asked the generalized question, "Have you kept the marriage covenants?" Lawyers were put in an ethically tough position, due to their cursory-only investigation. They had no direct knowledge of their clients' affairs, but in most cases they could make some pretty good guesses as to what was going on. The courts, however, accepted this approach and the world went on. If the lawyer inquired too far into the keeping of the marriage covenants, there could be disastrous results.

In the case of one young man from Middlebury, there appeared to be the makings of a rather straightforward divorce, with little property and few complications. His wife was not going to contest the divorce, had not filed a defense, and was not planning to be present for the hearing. I arrived at the Addison County Courthouse for what I expected to be a five-minute hearing. Judge Larrow, a Vergennes native who had practiced law in Burlington, was sitting on the bench. Ordinarily, Judge Larrow was rather liberal in granting divorces and I anticipated no complications. My client testified to the facts supporting his claim of intolerable severity. I then asked him the usual question, "Have you kept the marriage covenants?" He looked at me, and with a puzzled look said, "What do you mean?" I tried to explain by saying, "Have you been a good and faithful husband?" Not getting the hint, he said, "Well, what do you mean by a good and faithful husband?" At which point, Judge Larrow interposed and said, "Have you ever had sexual intercourse with anybody but your wife since you've been married?" He turned and looked at the judge, and in all innocence said, "Yes, once." The judge was as shocked by his answer as I was. He called me to the bench and suggested the last question and answer be stricken from the record and that I voluntarily dismiss the divorce. At the time adultery was still a felony in Vermont and my client had thus made a confession in open court to a crime. I immediately followed the court's instructions, took my client to the back room, and explained to him what had happened. He went away dazed, shaken, and still married.

I have often wondered about the ethics of the situation. Did I perform my duty as a lawyer by not preparing my client to give a favorable answer to the question of marriage covenants, despite the fact that he had, on a single occasion, committed adultery? Or had I failed my client by not giving him adequate instruction on how to give testimony that was necessary if he wanted to get a divorce? I have also considered the role of the judge in striking a confession of a felony from the record. For once a client had been totally candid with the court, and his candor was rewarded with the continuation of an unwanted marriage. The one good side of this story was that when the state of Vermont considered the divorce reform legislation in 1971, I appeared before the legislature and recounted this case. It played a part in the passage of the legislation abolishing the doctrine of recrimination.

Thousands of divorces have taken place in the Addison County Courthouse. Each one of these was a result of a failed marriage and each one brought to the courthouse stories of frustration and unhappiness. There is no such thing as a simple divorce or one free of emotional drains on the parties. Oftentimes the worst in a person comes out in these proceedings. Anger and a desire for revenge sometimes overcome good sense and a need for the parties to get on with their lives. Negotiations over property can escalate to battles at every level. One technique parties often use is to figure out what piece of property is the most important to the other person, and then insist upon keeping it when the marital assets are divided—even if that particular property is of no value to the determined spouse. Sometimes the parties are fighting about real money, and other times the dispute is about things that are truly mundane.

On one occasion, Jim Foley and I were negotiating with our clients concerning the division of marital property. The marriage had been relatively brief and the parties were entitled to an equal division of their assets. A master list was made up of all the property. Jim and I and our respective clients sat down in one room and went through a division of all the personal property. This included last year's snow tires, some cedar boards that were left over from a building project, and the like. We finally got down to the point where we thought we had an agreement about everything on the list. At this point, however, my client crossed her arms, looked across the table, and said, "What about the canned tomatoes?" Thankfully, Jim had enough control over his client to get him to agree my client could have the canned tomatoes.

The personal property in another situation was a horse owned by the wife. The horse was being kept at the farm where her husband worked and lived. At the same time, the husband's lover was living on this farm. Understandably, there was some friction between the estranged wife and the current lover. The wife's horse was a handsome white animal she had used to ride in local horse shows. She realized she would be unable to keep the horse, as she no longer lived on the farm, so she decided to sell it. One day she brought a buyer down to see the animal. On the night before the arrival of the wife with her potential buyer, the paramour got wind they were coming and painted black zebra stripes on the white horse. The consternation of the wife and the buyer when they found they were looking not at this beautiful white show horse but at what appeared to be a zebra did not increase the feeling of goodwill among the parties.

In another case of a rather acrimonious divorce, the parties had resolved all issues except for half a dozen items of personal property. The wife insisted upon a brass clock that was in the possession of the husband. The actual value of the clock was no more than fifty dollars, but she attached a certain sentimental value to it. The husband was adamant about not giving it up. Finally, as they were about to walk into the courtroom for the hearing, he reluctantly agreed to sign a stipulation awarding the clock to the wife. The divorce was granted, the final order was signed by the court, and each party had accepted service of a copy of the order that awarded the clock to the wife. But her problems were not over: during the next two months the wife made contact on a weekly basis with her ex-husband to arrange to pick up the clock. He continued to stonewall her, refusing to turn over the clock. Eventually, out of pure frustration, she brought a petition for contempt of court in the Addison Family Court, charging her ex-husband with deliberately and intentionally refusing to surrender the clock, and asking the court to order him to be jailed until he complied.

John Kellner, who had been the husband's attorney throughout the proceedings, was asked to go to court with him for the contempt hearing. The legal fees involved would far exceed any market value the clock might have. Kellner berated his client, "Why don't you follow the order and turn over the clock?" The husband, embarrassed, shrugged his shoulders sheepishly and replied, "John, do you remember last summer when things were so nasty between my wife and myself? Well, I got so mad I took the damn clock out in the woods and shot it."

14. Highways-to-Taxes-to-Horses

Part of the history of the Addison County Courthouse and the trials that were held in it evolved out of the activities of the Vermont Department of Transportation and its predecessor, the Vermont Highway Department. From time to time, the highway department decided to improve the state highways. Such projects required the state to initiate a "necessity proceeding" to condemn adjacent land, taking it involuntarily from its owner in order to give the road-makers room to accomplish what they desired. There were procedures to pay the landowner for the taking, in accordance with the Fifth Amendment of the U.S. Constitution, which provides:

"Nor shall private property be taken for public use, without just compensation."

A necessity hearing requires the state to show it is in the best

129

interest of the public to take private lands for a public purpose. The court would determine whether in fact the public purpose was served by taking the private lands the highway department requested. It was understood that the highway department would almost always win the necessity hearings. Over the years, the highway department appraisers took the position that the privately owned land was worth virtually nothing. This resulted in large numbers of appeals to the county court to determine what would be just and fair compensation to the owners who had had their lands taken.

There are people who are uncomfortable with the provision that the government can take private property for its own use, merely upon paying the owner just compensation. That, however, is the law, and the only right of redress an individual has is to challenge the amount of compensation. This has made for some interesting trials.

In the late 1950s there were substantial road improvements south of Middlebury on Route 7. From time to time thereafter there were improvements to Route 7 and Route 22A, each of which required a necessity hearing.

In connection with the Route 7 improvements of the late 1950s, Jack Conley in one case argued that the highway department was not much different from a bunch of Nazis; he claimed that the jury should have no sympathy with the state in these matters and that the landowner should be awarded whatever the landowner felt was the appropriate compensation. While Conley's position may have been a bit of a stretch, I know of no case in Addison County where the jury felt the award suggested by the state was adequate. Additional compensation ranged from a few hundred dollars to more than ten times what the state had initially awarded.

During the 1980s the State of Vermont took on a highway project to improve Route 7 north of Middlebury, running through New Haven. The project was sufficiently large to require approval under Act 250, the environmental act passed in the early 1970s, which stipulates that the district commission, and perhaps ultimately the state commission, approve any development involving a substantial block of acreage before it can go forward. The highway department was not exempt.

Steps to create a "bigger and better" Route 7 north of Middlebury commenced with an administrative procedure called a corridor hearing. This attempted to fit the particular highway project into the long-range plans for the highway department in moving traffic through the State of Vermont. The hearings were held at Beeman Academy, a part of the town of New Haven's school system. The State of Vermont was represented by Jim Hirsch of the attorney general's office. Great maps were laid out and the process explained, inviting public comment. Unfortunately, public comment was just that and had little effect on the state's ability to proceed.

The second step concerned Act 250. In this case, there were several facts that made the hearing more than perfunctory. The stretch of Route 7 between the two roads leading east from Route 7 to New Haven Village contained several operating dairy farms. One of the considerations in an Act 250 proceeding is the effect the development will have on agricultural lands.

The state claimed it owned a six-rod right-of-way based upon an 1816 survey approved by the legislature that laid out the turnpike leading from Middlebury to Vergennes. Based on the survey, the state claimed it had title to land underneath the west side of several barns belonging to the farmers who were located along Route 7. The state's position put these dairy farmers in jeopardy of going out of business. The state claimed the barns of the various farmers were partially located upon the state's right-of-way and no matter how long the barns had been used by the farmers of their predecessors, title to the land underneath the barns remained with the state. At first blush the farmers appeared to be out of luck.

The Act 250 District Commission decided differently. Several hearings were held in the evening, again at Beeman Academy, and there was a sense of great frustration and consternation among the farmers who were fighting a project that threatened their livelihoods. The commission ruled that in order for the state to build the road, the state would have to build new barns for the farmers. The highway department appealed this decision to the state commission, which modified it so the project could go forward without the building of the new barns. But it directed the highway commission to adjust their plans to preserve the barns. Under federal regulations there was to be a thirty-foot clearway on each side of the traveled portion of the highway, and the existing barns would have intruded upon that clearway. In order to go forward with the building of the highway, the highway department obtained a waiver from federal authorities to allow the existing structures to remain in place. Thus, the situation was that the highway department claimed ownership of land underneath the west side of the barns, but they had to allow the barns to stand and continue to be used as barns.

Representing the farmers, we took the position that the state highway department did not own a six-rod right-of-way (99′), but only a three-rod right-of-way (49.5′), and that the barns as they existed did not encroach upon the highway's lands. This was critical to the farmers' compensation: If the State's position was correct, only minimal compensation would be called for. On the other hand, the farmers' position was that the highway department was taking their land underneath the barns, and though the farmers could continue to use the land to maintain their barns, they no longer owned it nor had the complete control over facilities they had previously enjoyed. We were set for litigation as to whether the highway department was right in their claimed six-rod right-of-way or whether the farmers were correct that the state had only a three-rod right-of-way.

David Pidgeon was one of the farmers involved and his case became the test case. But before getting into the particulars, a word about the 1816 survey on which the proceedings relied.

The survey commenced at the northwest corner of the old courthouse in Middlebury, at the time located in the area which is now the small square in front of the Middlebury Inn.

If you draw a theoretical line based upon the metes-and-bounds directions of the 1816 survey, leading north from Middlebury, you travel the current course of Route 7 about five miles. The exact perimeters were unknown, as no one knew exactly where the old courthouse stood, but by making certain assumptions based on the current centerline of Route 7, you can work backwards and obtain a fairly good idea of its site. However, when the survey went beyond the town line into New Haven, it showed the highway verging towards the west and down a path several hundred yards to the west of the existing Route 7. There was nothing on the ground—monuments or otherwise—to show that a highway had ever actually followed the route suggested by the survey.

Here enters into the picture a young man by the name of Dennis Hall. Hall was a carpenter who loved old buildings and was curious about their origins. He had befriended a Middlebury College art professor by the name of Arthur Healy. As a young man, Hall had watched Arthur do many water colors around Addison County and had also learned from him much of the architectural history of the barns in the area.

Hall was called as an expert witness in David Pidgeon's case. He testified that he had examined the Peck barn, the Cyr barn, and the Pidgeon barn, all of which encroached upon the highway's six-rod right-of-way but not upon the purported three-rod right-of-way. In examining the barns, he found that none of them had ridge poles: the cross timbers supporting the roof were joined to each other without one. The supporting members of the roof overlapped and were joined to each other and then held in place by the roof boards themselves. Hall also testified that the ridge pole was a building phenomenon that came to Addison County in about 1810: barns built afterwards were constructed with a ridge pole running down the ridge, with the beams fastened onto it. Thus the three barns in question must have been built prior to 1810. The court concluded that these barns must have been in existence prior to the 1816 survey. This finding, along with the existence of other monuments such as the stone walls, prevented the state from establishing its burden of proof that it was the owner of a six-rod right-of-way. This left the presumption of a three rod right-of-way in full force and increased substantially the farm owners' potential for greater damages.

The fact that no one ever challenged Mr. Hall's position concerning the history of the ridge poles in Vermont is quite interesting. This is the same Dennis Hall who made a videotape of "Champ," the Lake Champlain monster, and had the video published through various groups who supported the idea of the existence of the Lockness Monster as well as of Lake Champlain's "Champ." I, for one, accepted his testimony at face value: I was convinced that prior to 1810 barns were built without ridge poles and that after 1810 no self-respecting builder would have built a barn without them. I also believe in "Champ."

Next came the trials themselves. The testimony as to the farmers' damages amounted to a cross-examination of the state's witnesses, which intended to show they did not understand what the situation was all about, followed by the farmers' recitation of their opinions concerning the decrease in the value of their farms based upon the taking.

The first case was the Pidgeon trial, in which the jury returned a substantial increase over the state's award. The state appealed the verdict to the Vermont Supreme Court, challenging the trial court's right-of-way decision; however, the Supreme Court, while reversing the trial court's decision, said we were free to go forward with the other cases on the basis that we had been able to prove the state had only a three-rod right-of-way.[24]

The great success story coming out of these trials was that of the Cyr Farm. The Cyr Farm is located on both sides of Route 7 in the level stretch of highway as you come off the hill, heading north, and go past the road leading to New Haven Village. Donald Cyr was a typical taciturn Vermonter who could have posed for Grant Wood's famous painting "American Gothic." He testified that the value of his farm before the taking was $150,000 and its value after the taking was $100,000. The state's expert testified that the value of the farm had decreased by a mere few thousand dollars because of the taking. After closing arguments and the charge to the jury, the jury retired. About forty minutes later they came back with a verdict for the Cyrs in the amount of $53,000. How they arrived at that figure is still a mystery, as the best case for the Cyrs was a diminution in value of $50,000.00. The court adjusted the jury's award downward to $50,000, and the Cyrs eventually received that sum together with interest from the date of the taking calculated at the annual rate of 12%.

The other plaintiffs were awarded sums far in excess of the state-appraised losses, but no one approached the Cyrs' verdict of 106% of what they asked for.

The same Jim Hirsch who had been involved in the corridor hearings and the Act 250 hearings on behalf of the highway department also played a role in one of the more humorous cases ever tried in Addison County. This was a case brought by the Mastersons, who owned a farm near the south end of the runway leading to the Middlebury airport. The Vermont Department of Transportation had the responsibility for defending actions brought against this state airport.

On behalf of the Mastersons, attorney Gerard Trudeau brought an action against the state claiming the airport was violating the rights of his clients, who owned a horse farm in the line of air traffic. This was a nuisance claim charging that incoming, low-flying planes disturbed their use of the property, scared their horses, and devalued their property on the market. During witness questioning, Attorney Hirsch challenged the concept of whether the horses would in fact see the airplanes and be frightened of them. To prove his point, he got down on his hands and knees, pretending he was a horse being disturbed by an airplane. He did everything but neigh. It was a sight to behold. Despite his antics, which some felt almost lost the case for the state, the jury decided air transportation was here to stay and the Mastersons would have to bear the burden of low-flying planes without any compensation from the state.

In 1974, a one-acre lot of land located in Panton on the west side of Route 22A went on the market. The owner was asking the very reasonable price of $1,000 for the lot, which had a view of the Adirondacks in New York State. Some years before, a close friend of mine from Middlebury named Bill Rule had brought me in on an opportunity he had to purchase a deer camp in Ripton. We bought it together and it turned out to be a very advantageous purchase. As a turnaround, I asked Bill if he wanted to purchase a one-half interest in the Panton lot. He did, and we took title to the land in both of our names. We held the land for a little over one year and were then able to sell it at a price of $2,500.

In 1973 Vermont passed a land-gains tax. This tax was intended to limit speculators' buying up Vermont lands, subdividing them, and then selling them at large profits. The way the tax worked was that in raw-land sales the tax on the first 100% of profit was 30%; in the next bracket of up to 200% profit, the rate was 45%; and in the third bracket, any profit over 200% was taxed at 60%. The percentages of tax for each bracket were reduced by one-sixth for each year the property was held before the resale. Thus, if a speculator actually held the land for six years, there would be no land-gains tax. If it was held for only three years, the tax rate was cut in half for each bracket.

I had always assumed the tax department would take look at the profit on the first 100%, figure out the appropriate tax, and then in the next 100-200% bracket use the higher percentage. If the profit was over 200%, my thinking was they would tax the excess using the highest tax percentage and then add the taxes in each bracket to come up with the total tax due. In trying to get an advance clearance of the paperwork from the tax department, I found out to my chagrin that that was not the way they were interpreting the law. Rather than treating it as a graduated bracket tax, the tax department treated it as a flat tax: and once you crossed into a higher bracket, all profits were taxed at the higher rate. This meant that if you bought a piece of property for $100.00 and sold it for $200.00 the next day, your tax would be $30.00. However, if you had the good fortune to sell it for $201.00, your tax would be $45.45. It seemed quite obvious to me that this did not make sense and that the interpretation of the tax department was in error.

When the tax department rejected my land-gains returns, I followed the statutory procedure for an administrative appeal to the commissioner of taxes. The actual amount at stake for Bill Rule and me turned out to be about $185. The methods of calculation, however, had a large potential effect on the revenues of the state as there had been no previous court determination as to how the tax should be calculated. In all previous cases involving profits into the second or third bracket, there were other complications such as allocations for buildings, and either they had reached a compromise adjustment or the tax had been paid. It appeared that our modest investment in a small lot was going to be a case of first impression before the tax commissioner.

The commissioner was a lawyer and an old friend of mine, and I thought it would be fun to point out to him how ridiculous his department had become in interpreting a tax this way, leading to such inappropriate results. An informal hearing was held in the commissioner's office in Montpelier, and everyone cooperated so that it could be on a day when I had other business in Montpelier and did not require a special trip just for this case, considering the size of the sum at stake.

In making my presentation I found the commissioner less than supportive of my position and quite concerned that I was trying to overturn a long-established policy of interpretation of his department over a mere $185. In a written decision a week later, he ruled that my position was incorrect and that this indeed was a flat tax where there was only one percentage rate to be charged against the gain, and that percentage rate was determined by the tax rate in the highest applicable bracket. This, in his opinion, was the intent of the legislature, even though it meant that a higher resale price could trigger a lesser net to the seller.

The commissioner's decision really upset me. I thought it was totally illogical. Furthermore, they were taking advantage of the situation because there was such a small sum at stake the commissioner assumed his opinion would be the end of it. To me it was more than the dollars and cents involved, it was a serious point of principle; and I was damned well not going to let the tax commissioner have the last word on this subject.

I filed an appeal in the Addison Superior Court to challenge the commissioner's interpretation of the tax. A hearing was set a couple of months later before Judge Wynn Underwood. Once again I patiently set out the straightforward facts of the situation and pointed out the illogical results of the state's interpretation. In full confidence of the correctness of my position, I rested my case and Underwood took it under advisement. Two weeks later I received in the mail the judge's opinion affirming that of the commissioner of taxes. Now, I was really upset. The only alternative was an appeal to the Vermont Supreme Court.

When the supreme court set the case for oral argument, Bill Rule agreed to join me in a trip to Montpelier to watch the argument, based upon my promise to follow up on the argument with a good lunch accompanied by a drink or two. I was seated on the right side as one faces the bench and rose when the five justices filed into the court and took their seats at the front of the courtroom. Counsel for the tax department was seated to the left of the podium. The bailiff announced that the next hearing was to be *Langrock v. Vermont Department of Taxes.* The chief justice greeted us with a nod of his head and then said, "Mr. Langrock, you may proceed with your argument." I can't say what was going on in the minds of the members of the bench, but I was worried that they might be thinking what the hell are you doing here, Langrock, taking our time over $185. I went to the podium and said, "Being mindful of the old expression that he who represents himself has a fool for a client, I would prefer to have you think of me today as representing my partner, Bill Rule, who is sitting in the back of the room." That brought a chuckle from the court, and I was comforted that at least they had a sense of humor about the case rather than being frustrated at what they might have viewed as a trifle.

The actual legislative history surrounding the act was rather sparse. It had been enacted in haste during the Salmon administration as a quick-moving stopgap measure to try to put some pressure on speculators who appeared to be running rampant. There was nothing in the legislative record that raised the particular question of how the tax was to be applied in a situation like this. I presented my arguments and showed the incongruous results that would occur if the state's interpretation were followed. The state argued the tax had been in effect for several years and now was being challenged for the first time, all over a mere $185, and said deference should be given to the department of taxes in its interpretation.

Two months later I received a per curium decision of the Vermont Supreme Court, a short opinion that states the reasoning of the court's decision in a straightforward way and is typically used in cases where the result is quite clear. It is presented more in memo form than as a lengthy judicial opinion, and it is not signed by any particular justice. This opinion was less than two pages in length. Reversing the trial court and the commissioner of taxes, it stated, "We find both in the favor of the taxpayer and in favor of common sense."[25]

For many years subsequent to that decision, the state's form for calculating the land-gains tax had on its back side a note. "In complicated cases please see *Langrock v. Vermont Department of Taxes*, 139 Vt. 108 (1980)." I have never known any other tax form to cite a supreme court decision, or any other appellate case, on the form itself, for purposes of interpreting a tax law. The various tax-reporting services picked up the case and it was reported in virtually all of the professional tax publications. In each article it was noted with incredulity that the case had gone all the way to the Vermont Supreme Court over $185.

In another tax case, in 1966 a client came in who was having a problem with the Internal Revenue Service. The IRS had done an examination of his bank deposits and determined that he had under-reported income and he owed additional taxes in the amount of about twenty-five thousand dollars. A brief discussion with him revealed that he was a horse trainer and cattle dealer, and unsophisticated in his bookkeeping records. Because of the fact that cattle and horses were bought and sold with cash, as well as with checks, checks that sometimes bounced and were redeposited, the government had engaged in double counting and in fact the man had not under-reported his income.

I told him I wanted a retainer of five hundred dollars to represent him in connection with his tax problems. He told me that he would like me to represent him, but he did not have five hundred dollars, and had no way of getting the money. He did go on to say, however, that he had a wonderful standardbred trotting filly by the name of High Missy he was training at Saratoga and she happened to be worth just one thousand dollars. Within fifteen minutes I called my secretary into the office, had her draw up papers that resulted in the transfer to me of a one-half interest in High Missy; papers to hire my client back as the trainer of my just-acquired one-half interest in High Missy; a check for the first month's training expenses running from me to my client; and requests for various forms so I could become a member of the United States Trotting Association and licensed by the State of New York as a harness-race-horse owner.

My secretary later talked to me and shook her head saying that she thought when people retained our office, they were supposed to pay us money and not the reverse.

High Missy never made it to the races, but I got hooked on harness racing and have been involved ever since that day. I worked my way up from a fair license, for driving at county fairs, to a full pari-mutuel license, which allows me to drive at any track in the world. While I am still waiting for the brass ring of that super horse to come along, I have had the great pleasure of driving in hundreds of races in racetracks all over the east coast and even in the United Kingdom. In 1994 I had the fun of driving Salisbury Seth to four consecutive victories at the Rutland Fair. Most of the lawyers around the state, as well as virtually all of the court personnel, know I drive race horses. They sometimes even make a small wager on the horse that I am driving. The four consecutive wins at Rutland did a lot for my relationship with those investors.

One February I had to argue four cases in the Vermont Supreme Court in the course of a two-week period. Percival L. Shangraw was chief justice. He was a fan of harness racing and knew of my passion for the sport. When I stood up for the fourth argument, the assistant attorney general at the other table was a bit surprised when I started my argument by saying, "As I am sure the court is painfully aware, this is the fourth case I have argued here this term. I just wish to assure the court that there is no correlation between the number of cases being argued this term and the present lull in the racing season." Justice Shangraw chortled, the other justices smiled, and I still lost the case.

What happened to the tax case that got me involved in all of this? Well, we paid the tax requested through a refinancing of some properties and then brought suit for a refund. We used a net-worth theory in reverse. I offered evidence to the effect that my client was a horse trainer and cattle dealer, that he did not drink, gamble, or chase women, that his assets before the period of time of the tax liability were the same as afterwards, and that he obviously only made monies enough to live on during this period, which was far less than the government said he earned. We achieved a very favorable settlement. The client was Lee C. Tucker, and his son Dale Tucker is still my horse trainer and farm manager, more than thirty years later.

15. Catastrophic Injuries v. Middlebury College

O ver the years, the courthouse has seen its share of cases involving catastrophic injuries where the plaintiff attempts to obtain compensation for their injuries from persons who contributed to the cause of the injury in some way. One theme runs throughout these cases, and that is the amazing resiliency of the human spirit. You would think a person rendered a quadriplegic or paraplegic by an accident would be a bit sour on the world. The opposite seems to be the case. Severely injured individuals are surprisingly optimistic about the world and their role in it. To be sure, they are concerned about the course their case is taking, but they are often less demanding of the system than are those who are trying to get vindication for relatively small matters. Two examples come to mind.

The first of these cases involved Steve Harris. Steve was born and raised in Norwich, England, and studied at the University of Leicester. He migrated to the United States, fell in love with a young woman from Ripton, married her, stayed in Vermont, and found work as a carpenter. When we were putting on the first addition to our law offices on South Pleasant Street, around the corner from the courthouse, he worked on the job as a carpenter. He had a full head of red hair, and he was gregarious and hardworking.

Shortly after he and his wife were presented with their first child, Steve took on a carpentry job working for Bernard Newton to repair a cottage on the Breadloaf Campus of Middlebury College in Ripton. On the second floor of the cottage there was a porch deck which was surrounded by a wooden railing. The railing was constructed with a top board and a bottom board with slats running vertically between them. The top and bottom boards were attached to a post at the outside corner and the roof of the building on the building side. In an attempt to replace the flooring of the deck, Bernie partially dismantled the railing, taking out the bottom board and the vertical slats. This left intact the top board connected to the roof of the house and the corner posts.

Steve had been working on another project in the building and came out to visit with Bernie. While they were talking, he rested his backside against the railing. Unbeknownst to Steve, the coupling where the corner of the board met the building was completely rotted out, and the slight pressure he gave against the railing caused it to give way. He toppled over backwards and fell about nine feet to the porch below. Tragically, he landed on the back of his neck and broke it, and was rendered a quadriplegic, losing all of the functions of his lower extremities and a substantial portion of the functions of his upper extremities.

Bernie was covered by worker's compensation insurance, which paid Steve's medical bills and paid him, weekly, temporary total disability benefits amounting to tax-free payments of two-thirds of his wages. These weekly payments were to continue until he reached what is known as a medical end-result, which is a point where his medical situation is stabilized and has no real chance of further improvement. He would then be entitled to permanent total disability, which at that time would continue his wage payments for a total of 330 weeks, or a little over six years. The rest of his lost earnings and his loss of enjoyment of life would go uncompensated, unless an action could be brought against someone other than his employer.

A claim was brought against Middlebury College for failing to provide a safe place to work, citing the dangerous rotten condition which caused the railing to give way. While most of the facts were not in dispute, it would be a close call whether the injury should be blamed upon the college for the rotten railing or upon Steve himself for learning against the railing—whose tentative condition he could have easily noticed.

One of the elements of damage in the case was the lost earning capacity and lost earnings that Steve suffered as a result of the catastrophic injury. The worker's-compensation insurance carrier, which had covered his medical bills and the weekly stipend, was entitled by statute to reimbursement from any monies Steve might recover against Middlebury College. The carrier's interest was substantial and it became a major player in the course of the litigation—albeit behind the scenes.

In order to convince the jury that Steve's potential for earning should be based upon his education rather than on his salary as a carpenter in Vermont, it became necessary to go to England to take the deposition of the professor at the University of Leicester who knew Steve best.

Our first difficulty in scheduling the deposition was to find a court reporter in England. Our initial attempts to find one were unsuccessful. My partner, Jon Stahl, knew the firm of Davis, Polk in New York had a London office. He called the father of his best friend at college who was a partner at Davis, Polk to see how they arranged for court reporters in England. The response he got was not helpful. We were surprised when we received a bill from Davis, Polk at New York law-firm rates for this consultation. It showed the difference between a big-city practice and a firm in Vermont, such as ours, where this would have been handled as a matter of courtesy had the query been made to us.

While we were talking about our problems at court, Joan Giard, a court reporter we often employed, indicated that she might be interested in taking a combination vacation/business trip to the U.K. With our encouragement, she and her sister made arrangements to add to a vacation in London a trip to Leicester, to take the deposition from the professor. Joan, who is now married to District Court Judge James Cruicetti, and still active as a court reporter when she is not tending to her family, met me in London. J. Fred Carbine, Jr., of Rutland, one of the defense attorneys for Middlebury College, joined us, and we journeyed up to Leicester by train. It was a first for all three of us, and it did result in some useful information concerning Steve Harris's educational background, for the damage portion of the trial.

Back in Vermont, we had employed John Outwater, a professor of engineering at the University of Vermont. Early in John's career he discovered that an engineer who would be willing to act in court as an expert was much in demand in personal-injury cases. Over the years he testified as an expert for both plaintiffs and defendants on everything from metallurgy to ski-boot design to construction. In this particular case, he rendered an opinion that the rot at the end of the railing was the cause for the rail itself to give way. He said, given the angles and the way Steve had leaned on the rail, the railing would not have given way unless the wood was rotten.

We had hopes to "sugar off," or settle, the case. ("Sugar off," a Vermont term, comes from the process used to boil down maple sap for maple syrup—the ultimate sweetness.) Steve recognized that liability was uncertain at best, and he was willing to take a figure substantially discounted from the full potential damages of his case. Unfortunately, insurance politics got in the way. Middlebury College's insurance carrier was using two Rutland law firms: Ryan, Smith & Carbine and the law firm of J. Fred Carbine, Jr. Both firms were apparently concerned about the future business from the insurance company, and each was trying to impress the claims people at the company. They could agree on trying the case, but they were never agreeable to sitting down with us and the worker's-compensation carrier to work out a tripartite settlement in the best interest of all the parties. Some money was put on the table, but it was not enough of a differential from the monies that Steve would in any case receive from the worker's-compensation carrier to justify giving up the possibility of a much larger verdict.

During John Outwater's testimony, he leaned on the railing directly in front of the jury, which was of the same general style as the rail that had given way—though of a much sturdier construction. He leaned against the rail as the testimony indicated Steve had done, and this part of the courtroom structure itself became a part of the demonstrative evidence of the case, although it was not dismantled and did not follow the jury into the jury room as did the other physical evidence.

Presentation of evidence concluded, both sides made their arguments, and the judge gave his charge, which included the area of law called comparative negligence. If the jury found the college was negligent as a result of the rotten wood, it would have to determine whether Steve Harris was also negligent in leaning against the railing. If it found he was also negligent, it would then have to divide into percentage points the degree of negligence of both the college and Mr. Harris in causing the accident. If the college was 50% or more negligent, then the jury would calculate damages by multiplying the total damages by the percent of negligence attributed to the college. If the college was not negligent, or the jury decided that its negligence was less than 50%, Steve would take nothing. The jury commenced deliberation and the lawyers began their wait.

Waiting for a jury to render its decision is harrowing for a trial lawyer. The matter is completely out of the lawyer's hands. It is a time of high anxiety alleviated only by the fact that during the waiting time there is nothing better to do than swap war stories with the other lawyers. There is also a rule that most lawyers follow, which is that they never have anything to drink before they go to court. The one exception traditionally has been that while a jury is out the lawyers can retire to the nearest watering spot and reduce their continuing anxieties with a libation or two. In this case, we did just that. My colleague Fred Parker and I went down to Fire & Ice Restaurant, and after learning that the jury had themselves ordered dinner, we had a few drinks and ordered our dinner. Just as we were finishing the main course, we received a call that the jury had rendered a verdict. The tension returned immediately. In a case of this magnitude, not only is there anxiety for the client about obtaining funds that will provide for him for his life, but quite candidly, there is also the very real anxiety that this could be the end of a long journey of preparation and trial where the lawyer either takes nothing or earns a substantial fee.

We returned to the courthouse and the foreman of the jury handed the verdict form over to the court clerk, who then handed it to the judge. After reading it to himself, the judge handed it back to the clerk for reading in open court. The clerk read the interrogatories out loud. "Do you find that Middlebury College was negligent?" Answer: "Yes." "Do you find that the plaintiff, Stephen Harris, was also negligent?" Answer: "Yes." "If the answers to these questions are both yes, please divide the negligence between the two parties." The tension at this point was almost unbearable. I could count my pulse in my ears as my heart pumped in anticipation of the up or down that was to follow immediately. The clerk then read the division. "The jury finds that the defendant, Middlebury College, was 35 percent negligent and the plaintiff, Stephen Harris, 65 percent negligent." We had lost. Fred and I were despondent. I think the defendant was less despondent at this point, and accepted the jury verdict more readily than we did.

During the trial, we had raised several issues that would form the basis of an appeal. The appeal was filed, and shortly thereafter we were able to work out a settlement involving Middlebury College worker's-compensation and liability-insurance carriers. The settlement was approved by the Office of the Commissioner of Labor and Industry, which has to approve all worker's-compensation settlements. Steve Harris eventually received some substantial funds, although far less than we had hoped to be able to obtain for him.

The second case of catastrophic personal injury began when attorney James Foley, a lawyer practicing in Middlebury, was out doing his morning run on October 12, 1986. As he jogged down South Street, he saw a motionless form lying on the front lawn next to the porch of the Kappa Delta Rho fraternity. Foley investigated, and upon finding a young man unconscious but alive, he immediately called for help. The Middlebury Rescue Squad answered the call and found the young man in very serious condition. He was rushed off first to Porter Hospital in Middlebury and then on to the Medical Center in Burlington. The diagnosis was that he had sustained a brain stem injury from a fall, was suffering from hypothermia, and that as a result of the injuries he was paralyzed in all four extremities.

John Foley, a student from Portland, Maine, and no relation to Attorney Jim Foley who had found him, was a goalie on the Middlebury College "Panthers" hockey team. Sometime during the night he fell out of a third-floor window of the fraternity house, bounced off the porch roof below it, and then landed on the grass where he was discovered the next morning. There appeared to be some alcohol involvement, but no one knew exactly how much at that point.

After a long hospital stay, John Foley was transferred back home to Maine to undertake rehabilitation for his catastrophic injuries. His family retained Daniel Lilley, the noted Portland personal-injury lawyer. The statute of limitations was going to expire on the 12th day of October, 1989, three years from the date of the accident. Just one week before the statute expired, Lilley's office called us—to ask us to act as Vermont counsel in bringing a law suit against Middlebury College and the fraternity. We had little time to investigate, but based upon the representations made to us by Dan Lilley, we agreed and filed suit before the statute of limitations outlawed the claim. Our pleadings were general-notice pleadings, in which the complaint filed with the court simply said that an accident had happened, that the College and the fraternity were negligent, and that their negligence was a proximate cause of our client's injuries. No great specificity is required by our rules in this type of pleading, and none was made in our complaint.

The original theory that Dan Lilley had propounded was that alcohol had played a part in the accident, and as John Foley was underage and was drinking on campus, the College and fraternity should be responsible for his injuries due to their lack of proper supervision and enforcement of alcohol rules.

As we got into the case and examined the premises, we came to the conclusion that the real cause of the accident was the structure and design of the dormitory room from which John Foley fell.

In the 1970s Middlebury College came down hard on fraternities. The end result was that it abolished fraternities as they were then known on campus, and required all the fraternity houses to end the business of owning lodging facilities for students. In the case of the KDR fraternity, the college actually purchased the building that had been the fraternity house. The fraternity continued as a social club and leased back the facilities from the college. After acquiring the building, the college hired an architect to bring it up to the college's dormitory standards. An investigation into John Foley's accident indicated that after considerable partying at the fraternity, he had gone to bed in the room on the third floor. Sometime during the night he had gotten up, and in crossing the room had tripped or lost his balance and fallen against the wall near the window. The room was constructed so that it was like a chute heading towards the window. The window itself had a very low sill, only twenty-one inches from the floor. As Foley fell towards the window, he stretched out his arms, but because of the low sill he fell right through the screen and out the window. Foley's memory of exactly what had happened in the room was very vague, and he recalled only that his foot had caught on something like a cord, causing him to hurtle forward.

We contacted Ben Stein, an architect who had been involved in the design of many school buildings, and asked him to take a look at the situation. After he examined the room and its measurements, and architectural literature, he came to the conclusion that the cause of the accident was the defective design of the room. An examination of all the windows in the college dormitories indicated that this was the singularly most dangerous window on campus because of its location and its low sill. Based upon Stein's conclusions, we abandoned the notion that the college's responsibility was one of lack of supervision and enforcement of rules involving alcohol. We went forward instead on the allegation that the college's failure to provide a safe room for dormitory purposes was the cause of the accident. John Webber, an attorney from Rutland, was representing the fraternity, and he made an offer to settle KDR's responsibilities in this matter that, though modest, was acceptable. Once we adopted the theory of liability based upon the window defect, the strength of the case against the fraternity was rather weak; KDR no longer owned the building, was merely a lessee, and had no rights allowing it to dictate the design of the building.

The attorney for the college was Karen McAndrew. Karen, an experienced trial lawyer, was with the well-established Burlington firm of Dinse, Erdmann & Clapp, which traces its origins to Edmund & Austin, a partner of which, Warren Austin, became a U.S. Senator and served the United States as its first ambassador to the United Nations. Karen is married to Frederick Allen, chief justice of the Vermont Supreme Court from 1985 to 1997. Fred Allen is also the father, by his first marriage, of the wife of one of my partners, Martha Wool. As is often the case in Vermont, the lawyers knew each other socially, but in the courtroom they displayed different dimensions of cordiality.

In the course of pre-trial discovery, we all journeyed to Portland, Maine, so that the college could take the plaintiff's deposition. This event was scheduled at Dan Lilley's offices, and there, for the first time, I met my client. A more pleasant, cheerful young man could not be imagined. He had worked hard in rehabilitation and had achieved some minimal mobility in his limbs. He had regained sufficient use of his upper arms that he probably would have been eligible to obtain a driver's license to operate a specially equipped automobile. However, he was determined that he was not going to drive if he was to be dependent upon somebody at either end of the drive to assist him. He therefore, by sheer force of will, had learned to move himself on crutches, albeit at a very slow pace. With complete concentration, he could walk by swinging one foot a short distance, then leaning on the crutch for that foot, and then moving his other foot in a similar manner. This former hockey player was thus able to enter Dan Lilley's office under his own power on crutches, and his obvious determination made my heart go out to him.

John Foley's older brother had graduated from Middlebury, and one of John's goals was to earn a Middlebury degree himself. In fact, he was initially reluctant to sue Middlebury College, and it was only when he realized the college's insurance company had been receiving premiums from the college for the very purpose of paying such claims that he was willing to allow the litigation to go forward. Subsequent to the accident, he completed all the requirements for a degree at the University of Southern Maine. He hoped these credits could be transferred to Middlebury and that Middlebury would give him a degree. Middlebury, however, had a rule that in order to obtain a Middlebury degree, a student had to be in residence for the last semester. Given his medical condition and the facilities at Middlebury, this was an impossibility.

The deposition went forward and John acquitted himself well during the course of it. After its completion, I suggested to McAndrew that in his case the college might consider waiving the requirement of residency for the last six months, allowing John to reach his desired goal: a Middlebury College degree. The college's response through counsel was, "The college really isn't very happy about his bringing suit and I have doubts if they will waive the requirement." After seeing this young man deal with the tragic accident so admirably, I found it hard to believe the college would want to do anything but help him. A college degree from Middlebury would have meant a lot to him and it would have cost the college nothing.

By the time the case came up for trial, one other major event had occurred. The college's insurance carrier had gone bankrupt. The law provides that when an insurance carrier writing policies in Vermont goes bankrupt, a pool contributed to by the other active insurers kicks in. The statute protects both the injured person and the defendant, who, expecting continued coverage, no longer has it because of the bankruptcy. We were no longer dealing with an insurance company facing substantial exposure because of high-limit liability coverage; we were now dealing with a statutory pool that afforded a maximum recovery of $300,000. The college itself was now responsible for any verdict over $300,000.

The trial got underway in the Addison Superior Court in July, 1993. Much to our surprise, the president of Middlebury College, John McCardell, sat at counsel table throughout the proceedings.

We had expected a representative of the college to sit at counsel table, but did not expect that the president himself would take a big chunk out of his schedule to play an active role in the trial of this personal-injury claim.

The success of our case hinged substantially on the testimony of our expert architect, Ben Stein. I had known Ben for some thirty years, and I respected his abilities and judgments. He is a gregarious individual who likes to talk and who on occasion likes to drink quality single-malt scotch whiskey. He is also rather relaxed in his dress and demeanor. The day arrived for his testimony, and he met us at our office. Much to our chagrin, we noticed that the shoes he was wearing did not match: one was brown and the other black. This did not conform to the image we wanted to project before the jury. We pointed this out to Ben, but since there was not enough time for him to go home to Burlington and return to testify, we sent him down to Ames where he purchased a pair of inexpensive shoes. These shoes would not have won any awards for fashion, but at least they matched, and he was able to testify on the stand presenting a reasonably professional appearance.

As the case proceeded, we continued our negotiations with the other side. It was obvious that McAndrew, smelling a possible victory, wanted to see the case go to verdict. However, she was somewhat constrained by the financial risks to her clients—both the college and the insurance pool. The time came when she made an offer. My partner, John Kellner, who was trying the case with me, went into the back room with our client and his parents to discuss the offer. Kellner had been doing most of the negotiations and he was convinced that the other side had reached its limit.

John Foley was exhausted by the ordeal. Because the Addison County Courthouse had no elevator, getting to the second floor courtroom was a major problem in and of itself. So much for access to justice for a disabled person. John's parents were there to advise him, but the ultimate decision was his. Although the amount of the offer was not what we wanted for John, we thought it was the best we could get, and, weighing the dangers of losing the case, we thought it would be prudent for him to take the offer, and recommended that he do so.

John agreed, but he asked again whether, in addition to the dollars offered, we could get the college to cooperate in giving him a degree. John Kellner went out into the courtroom where he asked Attorney McAndrew to have Middlebury College reconsider giving

John Foley a degree by waiving the last semester's residency requirement. McAndrew said that she would have to consult with her client. She walked into the defendant's-counsel room and closed the door, leaving President McCardle sitting by himself in the courtroom. Kellner was concerned that the purpose of McAndrew's retreat to the counsel room was to make a telephone call to get authority to take off the table the dollar offer which our client had agreed to accept. (We found out later that this was exactly what she was trying to do.) Seeing McCardle still in the courtroom, Kellner realized that what was going on had nothing to do with the possibility of Foley receiving a Middlebury degree. He knocked on the door of the defense counsel's room. When he received no response, he opened the door, and told McAndrew that her settlement offer was accepted. McAndrew told him to leave the room, and he did so. Moments later, McAndrew emerged and told us that the offer was withdrawn.

We then asked for a hearing before the court outside the presence of the jury. We explained to the court that the defense had made an offer that we had accepted before it was withdrawn, and that we felt the case was settled. McAndrew took the position that since the offer was withdrawn, Middlebury College would not pay the sum and the case should resume. We responded that we would go forward, with the understanding that the case had been settled at an agreed figure, and that we were not waiving our rights to the contract of settlement by going forward. Judge Edward Cashman allowed us to proceed in that fashion.

At that point, we were riding fairly high. We figured if we concluded the case with a larger judgment, it would stand; but that on the other hand if we lost the case, we would still have a strong contract claim for the previously established settlement. Apparently McAndrew deduced our win-win situation. The next morning when we returned to court, she handed me a note, which read, "The defendant will pay you X dollars in full settlement of this claim. *This offer is open until 11:00 a.m.*" It was the same figure that we had previously agreed upon. After conferring with our client, we told McAndrew that he accepted the settlement, and the court was so notified. Under all the circumstances, we insisted upon placing the settlement on the record.

The judge came out of chambers onto the bench in open court but outside the presence of the jury. He indicated he had heard we had reached a settlement and wanted to verify that on the record. I addressed the court and told him it was my understanding the case was settled. The judge turned to Ms. McAndrew and asked if my understanding was correct. There was silence for a prolonged period, and finally the judge asked, "Have you reached a settlement or not?" Still no response from McAndrew. I interjected that McAndrew had given me a written offer that morning, stating the offer was open until 11:00 a.m., and that our client had accepted it. Finally, Ms. McAndrew acknowledged that, in fact, a settlement had been reached. The case was resolved. The actual figures of the settlement were kept confidential by agreement of the parties.

From that moment on, the sailing was smooth. The settlement was to be set in a special-interest trust that provided future benefits for John Foley without disturbing other entitlements for which he might be eligible as a matter of law. There were some minor matters to be cleared up at a later date, and Attorney Dan Lilley, who had sat with us throughout the course of the trial, and who had been involved in all of the trial decisions and settlement discussions, returned from Portland once again. This time he brought two bottles of wine, a 1966 Mouton Rothschild for John Kellner and a bottle of a 1960 Lafitte Rothschild for me. I shared John's bottle at a dinner with our wives, but the Lafitte Rothschild is still in my cellar waiting for the year 2010 when it will be fifty years old and I will have been at the bar fifty years.

Unfortunately, John Foley never got his degree from Middlebury College.

16. "Baby Peter"

People end up in courthouses because they have disputes they cannot resolve among themselves. Most often one side walks away a winner and one side a loser. Sometimes both walk away feeling they have lost. It is only on a rare occasion that both sides of a controversy walk away from the courthouse in a win-win situation. One of those occasions was the "Baby Peter" case.

In the years 1993 and 1994 there was a great deal of national publicity about the Baby Richard case and the Baby Jessica case. These were cases that pitted natural parents against potential adoptive parents. In both of these cases, long dragged-out legal battles took place and the general public felt the best interest of the children was being ignored.

In December of 1993, a young man by the name of Daniel

Harriman made an appointment with me. He told me this story. He was married, with two young daughters, and had been in the army. When he was stationed in Louisiana during the summer and fall of 1993, Harriman learned that his wife, who had remained in upstate New York, was pregnant. His wife had apparently left him for another man and there was a divorce in the making. Harriman had been unable to trace exactly what had happened with regard to his wife's pregnancy until he returned home in December of 1993. After doing some detective work on his own, he discovered his wife had given birth to a baby boy at the end of November, at Porter Hospital in Middlebury. He also learned the baby had been placed out for adoption. Harriman had never received any notice of the adoption proceeding.

Our office did a preliminary investigation and found that, in fact, a baby boy named Peter had been born to his wife on November 24, 1993, and had been turned over immediately for adoption to a couple from Vergennes by the name of McDurfee. Judge Chester Ketcham of the Addison Probate Court made the placement after the mother surrendered her rights to the child. This was done without notifying my client, based upon affidavits of the mother and her boyfriend that the child, while born in wedlock, was not my client's child but, rather, the boyfriend's child.

Dan took the position that if in fact the father was the boyfriend, he would not make any claim to the child, even though technically, having been born in wedlock the baby was Dan's. However, if this was biologically his son, Dan wanted to have the baby returned to him and to obtain custody.

As you can well imagine, there was great agitation when we entered our appearance on behalf of Mr. Harriman. The probate court contacted both Pam Marsh, the McDurfees' attorney, and Susan Fowler (who in 1994 was elected the probate judge in Chittenden County), who represented the mother and boyfriend. Everybody but my client believed the original affidavits were true and the initial thought was that my client was merely a troublemaker. Dan agreed to leave the child with the McDurfees until blood tests were given to all the parties, to determine the biological paternity. Blood-testing appointments were set up. My client appeared for his test, the adopting parents brought "Baby Peter" for his, but the mother and the boyfriend, the putative father, failed to show. A court order was issued requiring them to submit to the tests. This was finally accomplished and the reports from the laboratories indicated that my client had a better than 99% chance of being the biological father. Further, the tests absolutely excluded the boyfriend as the father. The McDurfees, who had a strong community-support group, had gone public with the situation, and they had raised funds to help them with legal fees. They refused to surrender "Baby Peter" to the natural father, and replaced Pam Marsh with Bill Meub, an attorney who had practiced in Middlebury for a considerable period of time before moving to Rutland. He was retained to procure an order to confirm the preliminary adoption placement as a final placement.

I felt very secure that there was no basis for the court to terminate my client's parental rights. He had proceeded diligently to search out where his son was. He had retained counsel within five or six weeks after the birth of the child and made his wishes known immediately. A certain amount of national attention focused on the case, and in an interview with National Public Radio I took the position that there was little doubt but that we would prevail in our legal quest to have the child returned to his father, Dan Harriman. Due to the delays in the blood-testing procedures and the change of counsel, it was early August, 1994, before the hearing came before the Addison Probate Court. The baby was now almost nine months old, and Harriman had never laid eyes on his son.

My client had been able to pay a $500 retainer, but beyond that he was tapped-out on his financial resources. The other side was in a better position and they were able to hire an expert, a professor at Harvard University who specialized in early childhood development and adoptions. The hearing was held in the main courtroom of the Addison County Courthouse behind locked doors. Under the Vermont statutes, adoption proceedings are closed to the public. Undaunted, the local and national press filled the courthouse corridors in anticipation of a newsbreak. It was a highly charged atmosphere.

In the closed proceeding the adoptive parents called their expert, Dr. Joyce McGuire Pavao. Before allowing her to testify as an expert, we challenged her credentials and potential bias in this matter. I was convinced this expert, like most experts, was a hired gun for one party and I wanted to do whatever I could to undermine her position.

Much to my surprise, when she started her substantive testimony, she was objective. She testified that it was critical for the child to have roots with his biological parents. Furthermore, it was important for him not to be removed from the secure environment of his first nine months. The expert added that if the child had been taken away at a much younger age, such as two or three months, there would be few problems resulting from the move. Likewise, if the child were older, the child could probably more easily adjust to such a move. She suggested that nine months of age was the worst time to move a child because it was at this point in the child's development that he was just learning to adapt to the maturing experience of parental separation and reunion. Removing the child from the adopting parents at this juncture could produce feelings of separation never to be resolved, and severe repercussions in his psychological development.

The court broke for a noon recess and we went back to our office. Sandwiches were ordered and we sat in my office discussing our strategies for the afternoon. My client had taken the expert testimony to heart. He was torn between his love for his son and his desire for custody, and not wanting to force a separation from the only parents the child had ever known. He was confused as to how to deal with his need to be a father to his son and to have a substantial role in raising the boy, and what might be actually best for his son. Before the trial, we had attempted to negotiate a settlement that would give my client custody of the child, with the adopting parents also playing a major role through visitation. The negotiations did not bear fruit. We were afraid to give up the child in return for an agreement that Harriman could see him on a regular basis, because once Dan's paternal rights were cut off, we had no legal mechanism for enforcing any such contact. We were at a total impasse.

While we were eating our sandwiches, Ren Barlow, an associate in our firm, offered a Solomon-like suggestion: "Why don't we try to cut this matter down the middle?" Ren proposed that we allow the adopting mother to become the actual mother on the birth certificate, with our client becoming the natural father on the birth certificate, as was his due. We could then enter into a custody agreement, much as in a divorce, where the mother would have primary physical and legal custody, but my client would have enforceable visitation rights as the natural father. The adopting father would play the role that a stepfather would ordinarily play. We quickly finished our lunch and, excited, went back to the courthouse.

Bill Meub was there, and I took him aside and told him the possible solution put forth by Ren. Recognizing that nobody could really win this case, Bill started working with his clients to see if we could reach a compromise along these lines. After about an hour of trying to put things on paper, we were able to reach a settlement whereby Mrs. McDurfee would become the natural mother on the birth certificate, my client would become the natural father on the birth certificate, the child's name would be changed to Peter Harriman McDurfee, and we would enter into a stipulation giving primary custody, both legal and physical, to Mrs. McDurfee, with my client having enforceable visitation rights. The visitation rights would start slowly and work into a more significant role as time went on. Judge Ketcham approved this solution. We then went into family-court session, in the same courtroom but this time open to the world—including the press and its cameras—where Judge Edward Cashman put his blessing on the agreed custodial settlement. As the court announced its decision, the McDurfees jumped up with smiles on their faces, their arms joyously in the air, a picture of which made the next day's front page of the *Boston Herald*. All the parties in the courtroom were hugging each other and the reporters were running for the phones.

Arrangements were made that day for my client to see his son for the first time, and "Baby Peter" gained an extended family rather than being torn from his adopting parents' arms. The case received much national attention, including an appearance by the McDurfees, "Baby Peter," my client, and me on *Good Morning America*, and appearances by my client and the McDurfees on various other television programs across the country.

The real payment for me as an attorney for my services in this case was certainly not the $500 retainer. When the *New York Times* wrote an editorial about the case entitled, "For Once the Baby Won," I felt proud to be a lawyer. This was one of those few occasions when good lawyering and deeply motivated, committed clients resulted in a win-win situation.

An incidental story coming out of the case: during the live broadcast of *Good Morning America*, the anchor asked Daniel Harriman and the McDurfees how they were going to decide on future critical issues, such as whether the boy would play pitcher or catcher when he was of Little-League age. I interrupted and said, "The boy is a Vermonter, he'll play hockey." Whether my prediction will come true is yet to be seen.

17. Illegal Drugs in Vermont

The war against illegal drugs arrived in Vermont in the late 1960s. When I served as state's attorney of Addison County from 1960 to 1965, I had no occasion to prosecute any person for possession or sale of an illegal drug. Marijuana grew wild at various places in the county; hemp was once raised here as a cash crop. No one harvested it or, as far as I knew, even recognized it. College students were still drinking beer rather than smoking grass or experimenting with hallucinogens.

In 1960, when I was running for state's attorney, I gave a talk to the Monkton Grange about the federal heroin-addiction treatment facilities at Lexington, Kentucky, and how I thought, both from a libertarian standpoint and from a medical standpoint, that drug addiction should be treated in a non-criminal fashion. The members of the Monkton Grange were not familiar with the use or abuse of opiates. They were not offended by my comments; they appeared pleased that I had come to talk to them. They cared insufficiently enough about the drug problem that I carried the Town of Monkton in the elections of 1960 and 1962. The use of illegal controlled substances, which began to appear in Vermont in the late 1960s, was first met with scant information and heavy penalties.

While Vermont never reached the draconian penalties of states like Virginia, where possession of a single joint resulted in a twenty-year sentence, it did start sending people to jail for simple possession of marijuana. LSD was to enter Vermont later, starting in the early 1970s. One night in the fall of 1971, a rally was held at Middlebury College in opposition to the war in Vietnam. One of the participants was a young college student who had never been in any trouble. On this particular evening he ingested a large quantity of LSD. Sometime after the rally, the ROTC building at Middlebury College was burned to the ground. This young man was charged with the offense of arson, and he became my client. His father was a well-respected officer in the armed forces whose old friend, a former officer in the Royal Canadian Air Force, was Dr. William Woodruff, who by the late 1950s had become the leading forensic psychiatrist in Vermont, playing a role on one side or the other in almost every case involving the defense of insanity. Usually he was thought of as being unsympathetic to the defense and a strong believer in the position that people should be and were in fact responsible for their actions. It was in that context that I had first encountered him in the Charles Barrett murder case mentioned earlier.

Having dealt with each other on several cases, we had developed a mutual respect and had, in fact, become quite good friends. On more than one occasion we sat together in a duck blind on the shores of Lake Champlain.

When the young man's father contacted Bill Woodruff, Bill suggested that he should obtain counsel and that I might be a person worth talking to in that capacity. In fact, the referral of the case to me might have been even a bit stronger than that. I was retained on the young man's behalf, and at arraignment we entered a plea of not guilty by reason of temporary insanity. In Vermont there is actually no such plea as temporary insanity. The court treated the plea simply as a plea of not guilty by reason of insanity, and my use of "temporary" was regarded merely as hyperbole. The state immediately asked that my client be examined by a competent forensic psychiatrist and suggested Dr. William Woodruff. We agreed the referral was appropriate, and arrangements were made for the young man to see Dr. Woodruff. This was not done surreptitiously; I am sure the state's attorney was aware of my friendship with Dr. Woodruff and even aware Bill had played a role in sending this client my way. The state had full faith in his competence, as well they should have, and felt secure in referring this case to him. In due course Dr. Woodruff examined my client and filed his report.

The report said my client had voluntarily ingested LSD to such a level that it had freed up some underlying psychosis that he was then unable to control, so that when the building was set on fire, he was unable to conform his conduct to the laws of society. Therefore, the report continued, my client must be considered to have been legally insane at the time of the act and therefore not legally responsible for it. The report concluded that when the effects of the LSD wore off, my client's underlying psychological problems returned to acceptable limits, and he was not insane and not in need of any institutional treatment of any kind. When Dr. Woodruff's report was presented to the court, it was reluctantly accepted by both the state and the presiding judge. A dismissal of the criminal case was entered on the grounds of insanity, and, not requiring any treatment, the young man was released without any further proceeding. Criminal defense layers don't get any better results than this.

A footnote to the case occurred later when I referred to Dr. Woodruff as Vermont's leading forensic psychiatrist in an article for a law-school publication. After I mailed him a copy of the article, he sent me this response: "Why did you limit the part about being the leading forensic psychiatrist to just Vermont?"

LSD had an interesting history as a drug. Prior to the introduction of the various tranquilizers, such as Valium and Lithium, extraordinarily large numbers of people were locked in mental hospitals. LSD was being used in some hospitals as an experimental drug to cut through rapidly to the core of the patient's problem. The idea was that if a psychiatric illness could be thought of as an onion, psychoanalysis was the slow and costly process of peeling the skin off one layer at a time, whereas LSD allowed the treating physician to cut to the core of the onion quickly with a sharp knife. At about the same time as the tranquilizers were coming into their own, LSD was discovered by such people as Timothy Leary at Harvard to be a hallucinogen that could be used for hedonistic purposes. There then ensued a legal shuffle which brought LSD into the realm of illegal drugs the use of which would bring heavy penalties at the same time it was being abandoned in legitimate medical institutions.

Over a period of years, the combination of the widespread use of tranquilizers and the new practice of mainstreaming people who had mental deficits resulted in the virtual emptying of the state mental hospitals in Waterbury and Brattleboro and the Brandon Training School.

During this period of the late 1960s and early 1970s, Vermont became home not only to flower children but also to intellectuals who wished to experiment with LSD and other mind-altering substances. One group founded the Institute for Fundamentals in Lincoln and attracted a substantial following of very bright people.

One night, while having dinner at home with some company, I received a call from the state police. There had just been a raid at the Institute for Fundamentals and an individual arrested in the raid asked to talk to me. I excused myself from the table and went down to the State Police Barracks, where I met with one of the seven persons who had been arrested. Shortly thereafter, the group of seven decided to ignore the potential conflicts of a joint representation in order to have a unified defense, and I was hired as their lawyer. This unified defense evolved around questions of a possible violation of the Fourth Amendment in the search and seizure by the state police at the Institute's buildings.

I don't think I have ever represented a more elite group. It included a former college president, a Rhodes scholar, a former minister of health of Mexico, and four other people with either Ph.D.s or an equally impressive background of education and experience.

They had been experimenting with a particular drug that was used as a child's anesthetic. It was thought this anesthetic, when administered carefully, would give a simulation of a near-death experience. It induced a trance-like state for some substantial period of time.

Having picked up rumors about some strange goings on at the Institute, two undercover police officers decided to investigate. They approached the old farm building that housed the Institute and knocked at the door. Some of this experimentation was going on. The undercover police claimed to be interested in the work of the Institute and, more important, to have with them some wild mushrooms that had the capability of producing hallucinogenic effects. Based upon these representations, they were admitted to the house. Their observations while in the house resulted in their later executing an affidavit that formed the basis for a search warrant, which in turn formed the basis of the raid, which in turn resulted in the arrest of my clients.

I met with Dick English, who was then the state's attorney, to try to work out a disposition of the case. We developed the argument that the officers had perpetrated a fraud to gain access to the premises. Our contention was that this fraud required an invalidation of the affidavit, which would throw out the search warrant and suppress the evidence obtained in the raid. Without this evidence, the state would be unable to secure a conviction. At our meeting I used every technique I knew to convince Dick our legal position was correct. He did not buy it. On a second occasion, my partner, Fred Parker, and I tried to convince Dick our position was an appropriate analysis of the law. Dick maintained correctly there was no case where the United States Supreme Court had decided whether an entry by the officer in a case like this would invalidate a search warrant, and he further stated he didn't think they would decide our way if they were presented with a similar-fact situation. Fred and I argued the recent Supreme Court cases were all heading in our direction, and that if this case were before the United States Supreme Court, it would most certainly rule in our favor. Still no luck.

I went back to Dick English a third time, again making the argument that our position was obviously where the U.S. Supreme Court was heading. Dick appeared immovable n his position and it looked as if we were heading to a legal battle rather than to resolution of the cases. I finally said, "Well, if you won't take my analysis of the matter, whose analysis would you take?" I looked up on the bookshelf behind Dick and I noticed a reference book on criminal law written by LaFave and Scott, the most respected and widely read book in the field. I pointed at it and said, "If Wayne LaFave agrees, will you accept that?" Dick looked at me and conceded that if Wayne LaFave widely recognized as the outstanding constitutional scholar on such matters, stated the Supreme Court would adopt our position, he would seriously consider a negotiated plea. We had hoped for a disposition by a plea of guilty to simple possession of illegal drugs, so our defendants would avoid felony convictions or jail sentences.

In the early 1970s, I had the good fortune to work with Wayne LaFave in the preparation of the Uniform Rules of Criminal Procedure. I was a member of the National Conference of Commissioners on Uniform State Laws, which was charged with writing the rules and financed under a federal grant. Wayne LaFave, Jerry Israel, and Yale Kamisar—the three top professors in the criminal-procedure field—served as advisors to our group. Between 1970 and 1973, we met for a three-day weekend every six weeks to analyze the drafts of the proposed rules. Since Wayne and I are both early risers, we shared many breakfasts together, and we became good friends.

I thought I had an inkling as to how Wayne would come out on which way the Supreme Court would probably rule. We decided I would call Wayne and ask if he would be willing to hear the facts of our case and then render an opinion on how he thought the Supreme Court would decide the question. I went back to my office, called Wayne, asked if I could hire him as a consultant, and laid out the plan: State's Attorney Dick English and I would both get on the phone, and we would lay out factual background for both sides. Then Wayne would give his opinion. Wayne agreed to the procedure with the caveat that he would not accept a consulting fee; he preferred to work out of friendship—and I am sure out of curiosity.

Dick came over to our offices to make the call to Wayne. At the time, speaker phones were rare, and we didn't have one. Dick was in one room on an extension, and I was in my own office on my phone. Once we had connected with Wayne, we outlined the facts to the satisfaction of both sides. I waited in excited anticipation for Wayne to tell us how right I was in my assessment of the Supreme Court's probable position. Wayne analyzed the situation, and, to my chagrin, without hesitation made a prediction that the Supreme Court would come out exactly where Dick English maintained it would. I thanked him very much, hung up the phone, and walked out of my office. Dick English walked out of the other office at the same time with a broad smile on his face. Seeing him, I laughed and said, "So much for my legal abilities, but you've got to give me one for integrity." Dick also laughed and told me that after agreeing to the call, he thought he had been set up; he was both surprised and pleased with the conversation and its results.

I decided to forget about going forward in an attempt to suppress the evidence obtained in the raid and concentrated instead on the people aspects of the case. Dick, recognizing the inherent curiosity of intellectual people and the draconian potential of the drug laws, finally agreed to a solution very close to the one we originally sought. The state was well served, the clients were well served, and the only casualty was my reputation as a constitutional scholar.

The Zucchini Defense

Goshen, Vermont, is the most rural town in Addison County, lying in the southeast corner of the county and consisting primarily of land that belongs to the Green Mountain National Forest. The number of registered voters in the town in the early 1970s was about fifty. To this town came a wonderfully likable, friendly individual—a good worker, and a good father and husband. He was Peter Tonzini, a native of Italy, who had been in this country since his teens. He had one tragic flaw: he was addicted to marijuana. His wife, Anna Marie, was elected town clerk, and the Tonzinis were considered substantial members of the community who contributed to the warmth and unusual mixture of this mountain town.

A rumor circulated that Peter had on occasion grown some marijuana for his own use and had been generous with some of his crop with his friends. The state police got wind of this rumor and obtained sufficient information to convince a judge to sign a search warrant. Among the police officers executing the search warrant were two state police officers, Wayne Heath and James Lilly. (On his retirement from the State Police force, Wayne became an investigator for our office. Both Wayne and Jim later were elected as the county side judges and were serving on the bench at the Addison County Courthouse at the time it was closed in 1996.) The raid on the Tonzini home resulted in a seizure of what was proclaimed in the press to be a large cache of marijuana numbering hundreds of plants. Actually, the state police had counted each drying branch of a plant as a separate plant, and the real number of plants seized was really only about twenty-five. During the search the police discovered and impounded Peter Tonzini's collection of firearms.

Peter was a deer hunter and had several rifles. Unfortunately for him, one of his guns was an assault rifle fitted with an oversize clip. The state police posed for press photos with a pile of marijuana and the several guns, featuring the assault rifle with the elongated cartridge magazine inserted backwards so it looked like a machine gun. These pictures made the front pages of all local papers. The fact that the marijuana was found in the Tonzini home resulted in Anna Marie's arrest as well, even though she herself never used marijuana. A great deal of publicity surrounded the case, in part because of the photographs and in part because Mrs. Tonzini was the town clerk.

Our office represented Peter, and Missi Smith represented Mrs. Tonzini. After long and arduous negotiation, the state was willing to cut a deal setting an upward limit on Peter's sentence, but only on the condition that Mrs. Tonzini pleaded guilty as well—albeit with the understanding that she would get probation and not go to jail. The time came when Peter appeared before Judge Frank Mahady for sentencing, and we unleashed the zucchini defense.

The zucchini defense is named after that wonderful garden vegetable that grows so abundantly in Vermont in the summer. There is a saying in Addison County that the only time you ever have to lock your car is during the month of August. If you don't, one of your neighbors is liable to fill it with zucchini. The substance of the argument to the court was that my client's growing of marijuana was solely for his own personal consumption and not for commercial purposes. While two dozen plants might seem like a lot when fully grown, when they started growing in a seed tray, they really appeared to be a very small quantity. No dedicated gardener can easily throw out a healthy plant, whether it be marijuana or zucchini. This invariably results in having more zucchini or marijuana than is actually needed. Vegetable gardeners always seem to have an over-abundance of zucchini, which they give to friends to use in everything from pickles to zucchini bread.

We compared this zucchini phenomenon to my client's horticultural success with marijuana. Tonzini had started with only a few seeds and had been extremely successful in growing them so that when the time came for harvest, he had more than he needed. He naturally gave the excess to those of his friends and neighbors who also happened to be marijuana users. We argued in Tonzini's defense that he had no commercial intention in growing the marijuana.

Judge Mahady took a dim view of Tonzini's conduct, but he concluded that despite the quantity this was not a commercial venture and my client's objective in growing marijuana was to have enough for himself. The judge treated the matter as a case regarding growth for personal use rather than for sale, and he sentenced Peter to probation instead of a long jail term. Tonzini was placed on probation, which allowed him to provide for his family, working as the very accomplished welder that he was. He had good support from his employer and from his neighbors, and most thought this was a just outcome.

As a result of the publicity, however, Tonzini's case was called to the attention of the immigration authorities. As a resident alien with a drug conviction, he was declared deportable. We ended up having many hearings in Boston before an immigration judge to have this classification waived. The judge, who was also of Italian descent, turned to my client at one of the hearings and said, "Stick to growing tomatoes—that's our vegetable."

Tonzini was finally granted a waiver so he could stay in this country with his family. Unfortunately, his addiction to marijuana was greater than his common sense: he was subsequently convicted in federal court for growing marijuana on National Forest lands. After serving a long federal sentence, he was deported to Italy, with his family joining him there.

This is a tragic commentary not only upon Peter Tonzini's lack of self control, but also, in my view, on our society's hypocrisy: the condemning of personal marijuana use, with such destructive repercussions for a family, while at the same time condoning and even making available through state stores the high-quality gin that I prefer in my martinis.

John Zaccaro—A Case of Selective Prosecution

No case ever drew more reporters to the Addison County Courthouse than a relatively minor one prosecuted in the late 1980s. A Middlebury College student was approached by a young woman who turned out to be an undercover police officer. The officer talked her way into this young man's apartment and persuaded him to sell her one quarter-gram of cocaine. He was arrested on the basis of this single sale.

Sometimes what would usually be a relatively small case takes on a life of its own. That was true here. What would ordinarily have been a relatively minor drug charge against a Middlebury College student instantly became an international headline grabber because the student was John Zaccaro, the son of Geraldine Ferraro, the 1984 Democratic candidate for vice president of the United States.

Zaccaro was defended by Charles Tetzlaff, who was later appointed U.S. attorney for the District of Vermont by President Clinton, and who now spends much of his time overseeing the prosecution of drug cases rather than in defending them. Charlie was assisted at various times by a team of New York and Massachusetts lawyers who were considered specialists on the constitutional questions of search and seizure, and who were hoping to suppress the evidence concerning the sale. The case was prosecuted by John Quinn, Addison County state's attorney.

Ms. Ferraro stood by her son and attempted to provide him

with the best defense possible. Initial efforts to dispose of the first-time offense as a misdemeanor were rebuffed. Unfortunately for young Zaccaro, the more big-city power that was brought in on his behalf, the more recalcitrant the state's attorney became. What would have been a routine suppression hearing became a major source of news, locally and across the country. When Geraldine Ferraro appeared on the Addison County Courthouse steps going to court with her son, the cameras were rolling. In 1986, cameras were not allowed in the courthouse itself, so the reporters, armed with microphones and television cameras, waited on the steps of the building and made constant attempts to elicit statements from the defendant, his mother, the lawyers, or anybody else they could grab.

Hearings were held on the motions to suppress, and these were decided against John Zaccaro. The defense argued that not only was this a case of selective prosecution, but the entry by the undercover agent into Mr. Zaccaro's home was illegal. An appeal was taken to the Vermont Supreme Court. That appeal was dismissed on procedural grounds. The case went to a jury trial and the defendant was convicted. The supreme court eventually affirmed the trial court's decision and the matter was remanded back to the Addison County Courthouse for sentencing.[26]

Once again, the cameras were out in full force, and under the glare of the media a jail sentence of five years was meted out, all but four months of it suspended, plus a requirement of substantial community service. This was not necessarily what would have been expected in the case of a first-time sale of a small quantity of cocaine to a supposed contemporary by a person who had no previous criminal record. A report of the Vermont Department of Corrections showed the sentence was tougher than ninety-seven percent of those imposed under similar or even more serious circumstances.

The newspapers would not let the matter die and followed through with coverage of the size and quality of the apartment Zaccaro's parents had rented for him in Burlington, where he would be held under house arrest. John completed his community service, and since he was no longer welcome at Middlebury, he withdrew and finished his college education in New York, went on to law school, and has been admitted to both the New York and New Jersey bars. On his return to New York, he continued to perform volunteer community service, and he has lived an exemplary life since then.

John Zaccaro's case may have been a precursor of other nationally publicized cases that have taken on lives unto themselves, not because of the acts charged, but because of the celebrity status of the persons involved.

The Alice B. Toklas Brownies

In 1960 the State of New York had a drinking age of eighteen and Vermont had a drinking age of twenty-one. This resulted in a nightly exodus of Vermonters to various drinking emporiums just across the border in New York, with the heaviest traffic flow on weekends. (In a different approach, the state of Illinois in 1960 had a drinking age of eighteen years for women and twenty-one years for men. Times change.)

By the time 1984 had rolled around, Vermont had lowered its drinking age from twenty-one to eighteen, and, accordingly, a wave of drinking establishments opened throughout the state. In college towns like Burlington and Middlebury, there were lots of new bars catering to the college crowd. The Rosebud, located in Middlebury between Main Street and Frog Hollow, just across from where the Frog Hollow Craft Center now stands, was a lively example.

Among the regulars at the Rosebud was a young Middlebury native named Larry Riley, dubbed "Nuffer." Nuffer had been a star football player at Middlebury Union High School. He had been one of the bigger and tougher linemen in the state. He liked to frequent the Rosebud and drink beers with the Middlebury College students. Unfortunately, after a few beers Nuffer enjoyed fighting with students more than he did drinking with them. As a result of his aggressive behavior, which had the effect of frightening Middlebury College students away, management barred him from the Rosebud.

Nuffer was an employee of Green Mountain Construction Company, which decided to hold its Christmas party at the Rosebud. The night of the party, the Rosebud closed its door to any outsiders; Nuffer assumed that he was free to attend the party as there would be no Middlebury College students present with whom he could exchange either beers or fists.

Nuffer and a fellow former high school football player, McAllister, prepared for the party. They baked some brownies of a variety sometimes known as Alice B. Toklas brownies—among their ingredients was a large quantity of hash, and we are not talking about corned beef hash. Nuffer and McAllister arrived at the party with a plate of these goodies and added them to the buffet.

Everybody was set for a good time.

Unfortunately, the Rosebud's owner recognized Nuffer. He approached Nuffer and said that although there were no college students present, he was banned, and he was asked to leave immediately. In one of his more agreeable moods, Nuffer replied that he didn't want any trouble and that he would gladly leave, but he was dammed sure going to finish his beer first. This conciliatory approach by Nuffer did not satisfy the owner, who immediately called the Middlebury Police Department.

At the very time this party was going on, Officers Art Ploof and Gary Munnett were enjoying dinner at Lockwood's Restaurant, around the corner on Merchants Row. They were waiting for dessert when they received the call. Officers Ploof and Munnett left the table immediately and proceeded to the Rosebud, arriving there within no more than two minutes from the time of the call. They walked in and found Nuffer sitting quietly at the bar finishing his beer. They told him in no uncertain terms that he would have to leave and they would be happy to escort him out the door. Nuffer agreed to go along, but as he left the restaurant, he passed the buffet, grabbed a couple of brownies, and put them into his pocket. Officer Ploof, who had been called away from dessert only minutes earlier, asked if he could have one too.

Nuffer was bewildered. He was faced with three choices: (1) No, (2) Yes, and (3) explain that the brownies were laced with hashish. Nuffer made what was in his mind the only logical choice and gave Ploof a brownie. Ploof promptly split it, half for himself and half for Munnett. Together Nuffer and the officers left the Rosebud and made their separate ways off into the night. Nuffer went to a party not connected with Green Mountain Construction, and the officers went back to their duty.

Things remained relatively quiet for a short period of time. Officer Ploof had a Middlebury Union High School student riding with him as a part of "Career Week." The student was about to get a view of a police officer's career that few persons have ever had the opportunity to observe.

Within minutes the magic ingredients of the brownies started to work. Officer Ploof and Officer Munnett had no idea what was happening to them. Ploof, who was accompanied by the high school student, stopped a young woman for speeding and requested her to follow him to the police station. This was an unusual procedure in itself, but when Ploof went right by the police station and drove into other sections of town, the would-be speeder decided not to follow and went on her own way. To this day no one knows the identity of the alleged speeder.

The police dispatcher became worried when she overheard Munnett and Ploof on the car radio talking about witches flying overhead in the town of Middlebury. The dispatcher suggested that together they report to the home of Chief Watson. Ploof and Munnett drove to Chief Watson's house. They actually drove right across his front lawn, leaving their cruiser on it. Munnett attempted to knock on the chief's front door, but was in fact knocking on the side of the house. The chief's son, upon hearing the noise, looked out the window and hollered to his dad, "There's a police cruiser on the front lawn!" The chief, thinking his son was joking, ignored the situation until the noise continued. He then looked out and verified that the two officers had indeed driven the cruiser onto his lawn and were knocking on the side of his house. The chief immediately figured something was seriously amiss and sent his officers to the hospital. Blood tests were run and showed high levels of THC, the active component of *cannabi*s and the substance sought after by users of marijuana and hashish. Chief Watson relieved the officers of their responsibilities for that night.

Later that week the police reconstruction of the evening's events pointed to the brownies at the Rosebud. Further investigation revealed that it was Nuffer and his friend McAllister who had brought the brownies to the party. Not surprisingly, Nuffer and McAllister were arrested and brought before the Addison District Court. The local press had a field day, as did the national press; *The New York Post* ran the headline: "Local Police Eat Brownies, Feel Like Dopes."

Larry "Nuffer" Riley retained our firm and McAllister retained Rob Keiner. It was a difficult case to negotiate. On one hand, police officers had unwittingly ingested hashish through a brownie that our client had given to them directly; on the other hand, one couldn't help laughing about the officers' predicament. We were eventually able to work out a plea agreement where Nuffer admitted his responsibilities in bringing the brownies to the party and received a serious sentence but was placed on probation.

The story doesn't end here. Officers Ploof and Munnett decided their reputation had been maligned as a result of the press coverage surrounding the incident, and they brought suit against McAllister and Nuffer. Ploof was represented by another member of the infamous bar class of 1960, Joseph O'Rourke of the old-line Rutland firm of Ryan, Smith & Carbine. Munnett was represented by Pat Burke, of Castleton. The suit was brought not only against McAllister and Nuffer, but also against Green Mountain Construction for allowing such shenanigans to go on at a Christmas party. Unlike Nuffer and McAllister, Green Mountain Construction had insurance that covered the claim, and the company was represented by another Rutland lawyer, John Paul Faignant.

He was well known to our office because he had successfully represented me personally in a malpractice suit.

AN ASIDE

I was once sued by a former divorce client who claimed I had not advised her appropriately of her rights to an appeal. She had had a rather short marriage and felt she had been deceived by her husband when she learned he had met and had an affair with another woman while arranging their wedding reception. The divorce had been a tempestuous one: she threw all his clothes in their swimming pool, and he used an ax to break down the bedroom door. In the later stages of the divorce, she picketed in front of his business with signs accusing him of a variety of sins. She brought suit against me pro se—representing herself without a lawyer and filing it on the last day before the statute of limitations expired. I was represented by Rutland lawyer John Paul Faignant. The case went to trial, and the time came when my former client had the opportunity to call me as a witness. At the very moment I took the stand, the Institutions Committee of the Vermont House of Representatives came into the courtroom in the course of their regular inspection of courthouse facilities. When they saw me on the stand being cross-examined by a layperson, obviously a disgruntled divorce client, they all sat in the back of the room and enjoyed the proceeding.

I had been picked as the scapegoat by my client for her frustrations arising out of the marriage. With her permission, we had actually already settled the case for a payment which was more than twice what the presiding judge had granted her at the trial—infinitely more than what the one sitting assistant judge wanted her to have, which was nothing at all. It was not surprising that the trial court decided in my favor; the decision was later affirmed by the Vermont Supreme Court.

On the day before the brownie trial, Officer Ploof made a wise decision and dismissed his claim. Officer Munnett, however, who was now the Chief of Police of Vergennes (known as the smallest city in the world—one mile square, the only city in Addison County), decided to push forward. The plaintiff's evidence concluded at the beginning of the second day of trial, and the court dismissed the claim against Green Mountain Construction, leaving John Paul Faignant free to go home. He didn't. John couldn't miss seeing the defendant's case and the closing arguments. He stayed in the courtroom as a spectator.

John Kellner, a young associate in our office, had handled the civil case all the way through on behalf of Nuffer. It was now Kellner's turn to put Nuffer on the stand. Nuffer acquitted himself well: he said he had made a mistake, that he was very sorry for it, that he had admitted his mistake by pleading guilty to a criminal charge, and that he had paid his debt to society. Kellner offered as evidence the regulations of the Middlebury Police Department, which forbid an officer to ask for or take anything of value for personal use. There was no exception in the rules for situations where the officers didn't get a chance to eat their dessert. Kellner showed that the request for the brownie was in direct violation of the Middlebury Police Department rules. Further evidence was offered that Munnett's reputation was already tarnished—he had on a previous occasion tried to elude his fellow officers by driving down a one-way street the wrong way at a high speed.

Chief Watson was called to the stand. He backed up his officer, saying that the events of the evening had no effect whatsoever on his valuation of Munnett's performance or, he thought, on his reputation. While the chief's testimony may have helped the morale of the Middlebury Police Department's personnel, it did nothing to augment Munnett's claim for damages.

The time came for closing arguments. Kellner reviewed his client's responsibility and suggested to the jury that they indeed find in favor of the police officer, but that, as the officer had not really been damaged in any way, they should restrict their award of damages to only $1. Although he was tempted to do so, Kellner did not suggest a counterclaim for the hedonistic pleasures the officer might have derived from the brownie.

The jury retired and returned a verdict an hour later. They found Nuffer liable, but they disagreed with Kellner's assessment of the damages, awarding Munnett zero dollars. As Nuffer and John left the courtroom, John turned to his client and said, "I'm sorry. I should never have asked them to award $1."

AN ASIDE

John Kellner is a graduate of the University of Vermont. Somewhere along the line he managed to get season tickets to the hockey games at the University of Vermont, which can be obtained in today's world only by the bequest of somebody who had them at the time of death. He recalls that at a UVM hockey game one night the next winter, he looked over and saw somebody trying to climb over the glass to get at a Harvard player who had given a rather hefty body check to a UVM player. Kellner recognized that it was none other than Nuffer. Nuffer did not make it over the glass; as he was trying, Kellner approached him and said, "Nuffer, if I buy you a brownie, will you sit down?"

18. Fish & Game Cases

From time to time fish and game cases have supplied a touch of humor and a sense of proportion to the criminal justice system in Vermont. However, the often-quoted maxim that it is easier to kill a person in Vermont and get away with it than it is to kill a deer out of season and get away with it is not true.

In 1963 I prosecuted a fish and game case involving a fellow named Edson. Two game wardens spotted Edson working a muskrat-trap line in the early spring. When Edson saw the wardens watching him from a distance, he headed in the other direction—straight to the town clerk's office where he purchased a trapping license. Later, when he was questioned by the two wardens, Edson produced the license, but he failed to convince them that it had been purchased before they spotted him. The wardens had picked up sev-

eral of Edson's traps and saw that the traps did not have the appropriate metal tags carrying Edson's name and address. Two informa-
tions were filed, one charging him with trapping without a license
and the second with using untagged traps.

Fish and game cases are often vigorously defended, not because
of the fines involved, and not because of the public reaction to the
commission of such crimes, but because the Commissioner of Fish
& Game suspends the right to obtain a hunting and fishing license
for up to three years as a result of a conviction. To this day, fishing
and hunting are the major sources of recreation for much of the
population of Addison County, and loss of the right to hunt and fish
is a terrible punishment. This was even truer in the 1960s.

Ezra Dike defended this case. On cross-examination the wardens admitted that Edson had produced a license bearing the same
date as the day on which he was charged with illegal trapping. In his
closing argument to the jury, Ezra Dike leaned across the outside
rail in front of the jury box, looked directly at the jurors, and said in
a disparaging tone, "Did you ever notice that those fish cops never
work alone—they always travel in packs or pairs, just like sheep-
killing dogs?"

Dike's rhetoric was sufficiently persuasive that the jury paid little attention to what time of day Mr. Edson bought his license. After
deliberating for about twenty minutes, they brought back a verdict
of not guilty.

That was not the end of the story. The trial on the second
charge, using unmarked traps, started immediately. The second jury
was drawn from the same panel of potential jurors, and there was
some duplication of jurors. This time the jury was out for almost an
hour before coming back with a verdict of guilty. Was it Ezra's
rhetoric in the first case or the fact that the jury carefully weighed
the evidence in both cases that caused what might appear at first
blush to be inconsistent verdicts? I would bet on the latter.

Some years later, the tables were turned. Ezra Dike was state's
attorney. I was defending a woman and three men who were
charged with shooting a deer by spotlight at night and out of season. In this case, the game wardens were lying in wait on the
Lincoln-Ripton Road when a car came by slowly enough to raise
their suspicions. They followed it at some distance without turning
on their headlights. As to what happened next, the game wardens
and my clients gave widely divergent accounts.

The morning after the incident, the woman called my office

with a request to discuss the possibility that she, her husband, and two friends were to be cited into court for taking a deer at night. All four of them came to my office. The woman claimed her husband had been driving over the mountain on Route 125 from Middlebury toward Hancock at night, when suddenly the game warden's flashing lights came on. She said he stopped her car, and the game wardens accused them of spotlighting and killing a deer.

When I asked her whether she had a spotlight in the car, she snapped her fingers and said, "By God, I just happened to have had one. It was a large square battery with a spotlight attached to the top." Asked if the light was on, she again snapped her fingers and said, "You know, it is kind of funny—it wasn't on, but when the game warden's flashing lights came on, my husband slammed on the brakes, the light fell off the front seat of the car, hitting its switch in the fall, and got turned on." I was beginning to think the game wardens might have a case.

There had been four people in the car and all of them were present in the office looking for me to represent them jointly. When asked if there was a gun in the car, the woman's husband, the senior male of the quartet, said, "By God, you know there was. I had been out squirrel hunting that day and it was on the back seat of the car." I followed this up with another question, "Was the gun loaded?" He responded, "You aren't gonna believe this, but when I went squirrel hunting, I forgot to take the bullet out of the chamber, and when the warden stopped us, it was loaded." I realized that my clients had a problem, but I asked whether in fact they had shot a deer. All four of them joined in unison and said, "No, we didn't shoot a deer." A few days later, all four of them received a citation from the game wardens.

On the day of the arraignment, the two wardens who filed the charges arrived at the courthouse, and I had a chance to visit with them before the hearing started. They told me this story: They had seen a car heading suspiciously slowly south on the Lincoln-Ripton Road, and they decided to follow it without their lights on. They continued to follow it for several miles before it turned east on Route 125, heading toward Hancock. They indicated that at every field a light was held out of the car window, illuminating the area from one end to the other. Eventually, as the car came to a field on Route 125, the light came on again, focused on a big buck, and temporarily blinded it. The wardens said a gun came out of the car window, and then they heard a shot, saw the flash of the rifle and watched the deer fall and the car continue east toward Hancock. At this point, the wardens said, they turned on their headlights and took after the car with lights flashing and sirens screening; within one mile, the car containing the four suspects stopped. The wardens suggested that the defendants were following the usual practice of people who shoot deer at night—driving on to make sure they were in the clear before returning to claim the meat. According to the wardens, the woman, who was rather large, jumped out of the car and started running toward the woods. The others remained in the car. The woman had taken the light with her and was trying to hide it under her skirt; she couldn't turn it off, so a silhouette of her piano-like legs was illuminated under the skirt. She was stopped short of the woods and all four were questioned. They claimed to know nothing about shooting a deer. The game wardens went back to the field and recovered a deer that had been shot with what appeared to be the same caliber rifle as they confiscated from my clients' car. At this point, I acknowledged that the hope of a complete defense of the case was somewhat diminished.

After talking to the wardens, I met with State's Attorney Dike. He indicated he would be willing to dismiss the charges against three of my clients if a guilty plea was submitted by the fourth. At that time the standard fine for taking an illegal deer was $100, added to which were court costs of $5.10.

I took my four clients into the attorneys' room in the northwest corner of the courthouse on the second floor and put the proposition to them. I said that all four could plead not guilty, or we could get this matter over with by one person entering a plea of guilty and paying the fine and costs totaling $105.10. I explained the case as the game wardens saw it and asked them again if in fact a deer had been taken. This time they nodded in agreement that in fact a deer had been shot, and then—once again in unison—they turned and said, "But I didn't shoot it." I suggested I was not going to play God; they would have to decide if they wanted to take the plea agreement and which one of the four was going to plead guilty. I left the room. A few minutes later they all emerged and the elder said, "Well, I'll plead guilty." I told him to go downstairs and pay the fine, and that Ezra Dike would then dismiss the other charges. At this point, the woman reached into her purse and pulled out a long rolled-up stocking. She proceeded to remove a wad of bills and count out $105, which she gave to her husband. He took a dime out of his pocket to make the requisite $105.10 and started toward the clerk's office. Before leaving, however, he turned to me and said, "I wonder how many deer it is going to take to make up for this." So much for specific deterrence.

A fish and game case that actually went to a jury trial was the case of the "bare-handed smelt catchers." One evening in early spring, when the smelt were running from Lake Dunmore into Sucker Brook, my client and two of his buddies took their car to the area near Branbury State park and parked it in a secluded spot. Wearing hip boots and armed with buckets and flashlights, they started up Sucker Brook. The smelt run was thick and they could simply reach in with their hands and scoop handfuls of the fish into their buckets. What they didn't know was that a game warden was lying in wait. He observed them starting up the stream and followed them cautiously, staying in the bushes.

There is a small bridge over Sucker Brook, and like Billy Goat Gruff, when the game warden came to it he snuck up onto it and waited for them to pass underneath him. Shortly, my client and two others came up the brook, scooping up smelt and filling their buckets, talking among themselves and joking back and forth as they passed directly underneath the warden waiting on the bridge. At this point, the warden turned on his flashlight and said, "What are you doing down there?" All three men disappeared into the brush on a dead run and were lost to the warden, who found himself in a very disadvantaged position on top of the bridge. He was able to recover only an empty bucket and a flashlight with the initials "W.S." on it.

He returned to his hiding place near the smelt catchers' parked car and waited for them to return. Several hours went by and a man came back to get his car. He was dressed in a sports coat with a shirt and tie. The warden accosted him and said, "Who are you and what are you doing here?" He identified himself and said he had been out to dinner with his wife and friends and they had dropped him off to pick up his vehicle. The warden said, "I recognize you. You were the one with the red hat." The man denied having any knowledge of what the warden was talking about, but he accepted the citation to appear at the Addison District Court on the charge of illegally catching smelt bare-handed.

He came to see me with the sketchy alibi about having been out to dinner with his wife. I told him I would be happy to represent him; that I had no compulsions about putting the state to its proof; and that perhaps we could prevail, based upon the question of an inadequate identification. I made it clear to him, however, that I would not allow him to take the stand and tell a contrived story. He agreed to this, and we went forward to a jury trial. By the time we got to trial, the game warden had convinced himself the flashlight with the initials W.S. and the plastic bucket he had confiscated had been carried by my client, the man who allegedly wore the red hat.

The state's case was based entirely upon the game warden's testimony. He related how he had been waiting by the side of the stream for potential smelt poachers such as had eventually arrived. He then told how he carefully followed them up the stream, staying a good distance away in the bushes so they could not know of his presence. He told about getting ahead of them and up on the bridge and waiting for them to come under the bridge before he turned on his light in an attempt to apprehend them. He said it was my client he saw carrying the bucket and flashlight, which had been offered into evidence as state exhibits #1 and #2. He further recalled my client was certainly the man who was wearing the red hat.

The cross-examination was rather short and to the point. I pointed out my client's initials were R.S., not W.S. I inquired if the warden was aware my client had a brother with the initials W.S. As both my client and his brother were known to the game warden for various reasons, he had to admit that, in fact, he did know there was such a brother, with the initials W.S. I asked one more question: "Do you know how much my client looks like his brother?" The warden said, "No." That ended the cross-examination.

The jury deliberated and my client was acquitted. Since all the smelt had apparently been returned to the stream in the alleged culprits' hasty departure from the scene, and as my client incurred substantial legal expenses in an effort to protect his hunting and fishing license, it might be suggested that this was not a true miscarriage of justice. The next spring my client went to Lake Bomoseen when the smelt were running—albeit not quite so thickly—but where catching them, by hand or otherwise, is not a crime.

John Eaton invented and held the patent on a wood chipper head. This invention allowed slabs of wood discarded in a sawmill operation to be converted into wood chips for use in the pulp and paper industry. John lived in Hancock, and as a result of the monies he made with his invention, he became, by Vermont standards, quite wealthy. He owned large tracts of land throughout the valley, which has as its center vein Vermont Route 100. He established a buffalo ranch in Granville and imported live bison from the West to inhabit the place. He built himself a home with an indoor/outdoor year-round swimming pool, located on the top of the mountain in the northwest corner of the junctions of Routes 125 and 100. His house had a spectacular view of the entire valley looking south.

John liked to party a bit and was not by any means adverse to taking a drink. In the fall of 1966, he decided to host a party at his home in Hancock during the opening weekend of deer-hunting season. Among the guests was a man named James M. Ballou. Ballou, a surgeon, lived in New Hampshire, where he served as a member of the New Hampshire Fish and Game Commission. Because of his position as a commissioner for New Hampshire, he was grated a special courtesy license by the governor of Vermont, which allowed him to hunt in Vermont without paying any fee.

During the course of the party, which took place on Friday night, November 11th, the day before the opening of deer season, someone suggested that a little camp meat might be appropriate. Camp meat, usually a young doe, is a prerogative to which some hunters believe they are entitled, although its acquisition is well outside the fish and game laws. Two of the other guests, Tom Bowen and Gerald Sherman, suggested Dr. Ballou accompany them in their quest for the contraband meat. In response to their question, "Can you run?," Ballou responded, "I can keep up with the best of them." The three of them took off in a pickup truck belonging to Bowen. Sherman was driving, with Dr. Ballou sitting in the middle, and Tom (John Eaton's son-in-law), on the far passenger side. Tom had a 300 Savage rifle on the floorboards under the seat. They drove around the back woods of Hancock, looking with their headlights at every open field in the hope of finding a deer.

At Newton Meadow they got lucky—or so they thought at the time. At the far end of the field stood a doe, frozen by the light. They drove into the field, Bowen fired a shot from the car, and the doe dropped dead with a bullet between her eyes. The neighbors called the police dispatcher and reported hearing the shot so the information could be relayed to the Fish & Game Department. Game Warden Gregory rushed to the scene in his Fish & Game cruiser. He turned on his flashing lights and blocked off the exit from the field. Bowen stayed with the truck, but Sherman, who had been standing beside the truck, vanished into the woods and into the night, not to be heard from for many, many hours. Dr. Ballou, who was a bit rotund, tried to follow Sherman's example. He ran about seventy-five yards, and then, panting, went down in the tall grass and brush at the edge of the field and tried to hide himself.

Warden Gregory had watched this entire proceeding. He recognized that in addition to the driver of the pickup, and the man who had run into the woods, he had one potential defendant lying down in the grass. He decided to concentrate on that person alone. Within minutes Gregory was joined by two other deputy wardens. They came over to Ballou, shined their flashlights, and saw that he was face down in the grass in an attempt to be invisible. The problem was the dead deer seventy-five feet behind him. Ballou was told he would be charged with illegally possessing a doe taken out of season by spotlighting. Ballou asked the wardens if he could pay a "fine" then and there to resolve the matter without any publicity. The wardens did not take kindly to this suggestion, and after finding out who Ballou was and where he was staying, they gave him a citation to appear in court.

At a court hearing, Ballou could have paid a $100 fine with a no-contest plea to the charge and gone back quietly to New Hampshire. The incident was now a matter of public record and he made the fateful decision to proclaim his innocence, alleging he was only a rider and had not participated in the taking of the deer.

Ballou hired John A. Burgess, a very bright lawyer who was then practicing in Montpelier.

AN ASIDE

Attorney John A. "Awful" Burgess must be differentiated from Attorney John S. Burgess who was from Brattleboro and who had been lieutenant governor of the state. John A. had graduated from Boston University in 1960 in the same class with F. Lee Bailey, and the two remained friends for years. Their friendship was somewhat strained when John, in California where he had moved his practice, went to jail for embezzling funds in the millions of dollars from his clients. In that same 1960 class of the Vermont Bar, besides John, Phyllis Armstrong, Joe O'Rourke, and me, there were six other persons, and one of them also spent time in jail for embezzling funds from a client. However, he did not leave Vermont to do it. Twenty percent of a single class of lawyers admitted to a state bar convicted of the felony of embezzlement! I've often wondered whether this qualifies for *The Guinness Book of Records.*

John Burgess knew he had a good thing by way of a paying client, and he recommended that Dr. Ballou defend the case all the way. Ezra Dike, the state's attorney of Addison County, did not usually lose sleep over fish-and-game charges, especially of bungled attempts to take camp meat. However, when he met with Ballou's defense, which proclaimed absolute innocence and placed all the blame on local persons, Ezra Dike got his hackles up. Ezra never had any concern about his win-loss record, and he was usually willing to give the little guy a break. However, if a person started to throw his weight around as if he were a big shot, Ezra became as tenacious a prosecutor as you could imagine. Burgess's approach to this case was exactly what was needed to bring out the tenacious aspects of Ezra's personality. Ezra was determined to get a conviction in the Ballou case, and to strengthen his position further he subpoenaed both Sherman and Bowen. They had the right to plead the Fifth Amendment prohibition against being forced to give evidence against themselves; Ezra granted immunity from prosecution so they would have to tell their entire story in court.

Trial was held in the Addison District Court, Judge William Burrage presiding. Bill had a reputation as a law-and-order judge. On one occasion, speaking before the Middlebury Rotary Club, he suggested, "Sometimes the state's case is presented so weakly, I have to act as an assistant prosecutor." Every dog has his day, and Burgess had his in this case. After all the evidence was presented, Burrage directed a verdict of not guilty, based on his finding that the state had failed to show Ballou was ever in possession of the deer.

Ezra asked for permission to appeal the case to the Vermont Supreme Court before judgment was entered, and Burrage granted the request. The local papers, which had been covering the trial because of Ballou's newly-acquired notoriety, had a field day criticizing how the court took the case away from the jury. Due to the press coverage of the case, the attorney general's office received numerous complaints of a miscarriage of justice. These usually took the form, "How come my son had to pay a fine for taking a deer and this big-shot doctor from New Hampshire can get away with it?"

As a result of the complaints, and also because Jim Oakes, the attorney general, may have distrusted the abilities of Ezra Dike,

Assistant Attorney General Alan Cheever was directed to take over the responsibilities of the appeal. (Later, Alan became a judge, and he still sits on the Superior Bench.) There was no way Ezra was going to allow "them dunderheads up in Montpelier" to run his office. Under the Vermont Constitution, the attorney general could not invade the jurisdiction of the state's attorney without the state's attorney's permission. Ezra was not about to agree to this and the attorney general's office was limited to filing a supplemental brief with the supreme court.

Sitting on the supreme court at that time was Associate Justice Milford Smith. Milford was "Hamp" Davis's father-in-law and also the author of a regular feature in the *Rutland Herald* which covered fish-and-game news. The column was entitled "Short Casts and Stray Shots." Smith was also the model for the character of the judge in Cornel Sheldon's *Tranquility Stories,* that wonderful collection of hunting anecdotes written by Vermont's first Fish & Game Commissioner. Given his particular interest and indeed expertise in the wildlife area, one would think the task of writing the opinion would have fallen to Smith's hands. It didn't.

The decision, handed down in February of 1968, was written by Perciville L. Shangraw.[27] With typical Vermont dry wit, "Shang," as he was fondly known by the bar, wrote a history of the escapade of the fateful Friday night, summing it up with the comment: "It can hardly be assumed that this excursion was intended only for target practice without the intention of gaining unlawful possession of a deer." The decision of the trial court was reversed, and the case was remanded to the district court for a new trial. Ezra Dike had won this round.

The second trial was transferred to the Chittenden District Court before Judge Edward "The Only" Costello. The state's case again consisted of the game wardens' testimony about what they saw happen, and how they found Dr. Ballou lying face down in the grass a short distance from the dead deer. The wardens also testified to Ballou's attempt to pay a fine right there in the field. Bowen and Sherman were called and they testified as to the escapades at Newton Meadow. They related the discussions about getting some camp meat and Ballou's comment that he could run with the best of them. It was obvious from their testimony that Ballou knew the purpose of the mission.

Ballou still maintained he was a mere passenger and had not intentionally participated in breaking the Vermont fish-and-game laws. In the course of his closing argument for the state, Ezra Dike turned to the jury and, mocking Ballou's defense, said, "Ladies and gentlemen, I just want you to know that Dr. Ballou would have you believe that he was just bellied down there in the swale grass for his health." The jury responded with smiles all around. Burgess, who had been a debating champion at the University of Vermont, was quite eloquent—especially in comparison to Ezra Dike's folksy approach. He went on at some length explaining why his client should be found not guilty. As he concluded his arguments, he pointed out that the state, which had made the first argument, would also have a chance at rebuttal, which gave the state an opportunity to make one more argument. He suggested the jury "should think of the arguments as a sandwich: remember, the meat of the sandwich is in the middle." Ezra's rebuttal was short and one of the most effective on record. 'Mr. Burgess is correct: the closing arguments in this case are like a sandwich—a baloney sandwich with the baloney in the middle."

Needless to say, Dr. Ballou was convicted and went back to New Hampshire with his tail between his legs. The incident could have been solved with a small fine and minimal publicity, but instead it consumed two years with two trials, a trip to the Vermont Supreme Court, substantial legal fees, and—what perhaps was the worst part—the papers mocking him as the surgeon fish-and-game commissioner from New Hampshire who had been found "bellied down in the swale grass."

Many deer-jackers use the same *modus operandi*—the drive-by shooting of a deer and the return to carry away their venison when the coast is clear. This technique gives them some protection in case a local resident hears the shot and calls the game warden. By the time the game warden gets to the scene, the hunters are well out of the way. By the time they come back to check out the situation, they've had a chance to remove their lights and guns from the car.

Sometimes these procedures or variations on the theme result in amusing stories. My partner, Mark Sperry, was once interviewing a client who had been cited for taking a deer illegally. The client told Mark he had shot a deer that was at the far end of a field covered with fresh snow. It was early evening and he left the area. When he came back, he was dropped off on foot; unfortunately he had kept his rifle with him, and while walking down the road, he was stopped by the game wardens who had already recovered the deer. They gave him a citation, calling for his appearance at the Addison County Courthouse. My partner asked him what he had told the game wardens. He told them that he had been in the area, "but I had nothing to do with the taking of the deer. I became lost in the woods and it was after dark before I found my bearings and walked out. It's just a coincidence that you found a deer near here." Mark responded, "That was kind of silly. The game wardens will go back and find out that there were no footsteps in the fresh snow that showed your coming out of the woods." To this the potential client responded, "Oh, don't worry. After they left, I went and walked backwards into the woods a half-mile." The case was eventually disposed of by an appropriate plea agreement.

On one other occasion two young men followed the same procedure. Going down a back road in the town of Goshen, they spotted a deer, shot it, and left the area. Arnold Magoon, the local game warden, who was about 6'4", saw them do it. It was rumored Magoon would walk five miles through the woods at night without a light in the hope of surprising a deer jacker. This night he was on foot because he had hidden his cruiser some distance away, and therefore he could not give immediate chase. So he decided to wait for the men's return. He went and lay down in a ditch in the vicinity of the area where he expected they would stop when they came back to get the deer. About a half-hour later they did return, and one of the young men got out of the car to go and fetch the deer. At this point, all 6'4" of Arnold Magoon rose out of the ditch and announced to the young man that he was under arrest. The young man, thinking probably Magoon was an apparition and he was being set upon by a ghost, took off down the road. Magoon followed in hot pursuit. They had gone a considerable distance, keeping an equal pace, when Magoon took his pistol from its holster and fired a warning shot in the air. He later recounted that this was a mistake, because once the gun was fired, the potential defendant acted like the roadrunner in a cartoon and sprinted an additional twenty-yard lead over Magoon. Fortunately for the warden, the culprit was not in the best of shape. He soon ran out of wind and fell into the clutches of Warden Magoon. He later pled guilty and was convicted of the original charge of illegally taking a deer at night by spotlight.

During the years I was state's attorney, I prosecuted the first fish-and-game violation for killing a moose this courthouse had ever seen. A dead moose had been found near Chatfield's clearing in South Lincoln. Arnold Magoon, who was a brand-new game warden at the time, tracked down the perpetrator of the crime. The man was arrested and entered a plea of guilty.

For most of the nineteenth century and well into the twentieth, the State of Vermont, including Addison County, consisted largely of open lands. At the time of the Civil War, approximately eighty percent of Vermont was clear, with only twenty percent in timber. As a result, moose were no longer native to Vermont (the last catamount was shot in Stafford in 1885), and the white-tail deer population was so diminished that, around the turn of the century, deer were brought in from Virginia to replenish the herd and save it from extinction.

In 1960 there were operating dairy farms in every town in the county, including the mountain towns of Lincoln, Ripton, and Goshen. However, over the years many of the mountain farms had declined—from profitable farming operations, to subsistence level, to abandonment—and much of this land had reverted to forest. With this change, an occasional moose migrated down from Quebec. The growth of the moose population has continued to expand to the point where we now have an open hunting season, albeit a limited one. However, in the early sixties a moose was a rare resident of the county, and the illegal shooting of moose was thought to be a major trespass of the fish-and-game laws. Instead of the usual fine that accompanied most violations of the fish-and-game laws, the culprit in this case was sentenced to a short stint in the Addison County Jail.

At the same time the new courthouse was being built in 1995, renovations were being done to the county jail. One day, a construction worker happened to take a close look at the old bench where generations of prisoners had sat, either awaiting their turn for trial or serving out short sentences. He realized that among the initial carved in the bench were his. He had cut them into the bench during his sentence for shooting the moose!

AN ASIDE

Arnold Magoon was later killed when a young man who was stopped for jacking a deer wrestled Magoon's flashlight away from him and then used it to strike him on the head.

When the man was in my office seeking representation on the charge of assaulting the officer, a call came in from State's Attorney John Liccardi with the news that Magoon had died as a result of this assault, and the charge was now murder. I put the phone down and told my client what had happened, and he literally seemed to shrink as he sat in his chair. He had had the good sense to realize that he had seriously hurt Magoon and instead of running from the scene had held the warden in his arms and called for help. These actions prevented an indictment for first-degree murder, and after waiving a jury trial the court had to decide whether he was guilty of second-degree murder or manslaughter. They decided on second-degree murder but handed down a moderate sentence of something less than ten years.

Late one afternoon I took a call from a man who was at the courthouse and who had been trying to reach my partner, Jon Stahl. He had just been arraigned on a charge of attempting to spotlight deer. My partner was quite ill and the call was referred to me. The man told me he had been arrested by a game warden and transported over the mountain from Hancock to Middlebury. He had been released without any bail, and the game warden who had arrested him agreed to give him a ride back to Hancock. The game warden obligingly brought him over to my office en route, where I was able to meet with him for about ten or fifteen minutes.

The story he told was that he and his buddy had been out raccoon hunting, carrying a light to spot the raccoons in the trees. Unfortunately, the light consisted of a large battery pack strapped to his waist with a fairly bright searchlight; this would have been illegal even for the hunting of raccoon. He indicated that his buddy was already being represented by my partner, Jon Stahl, and he asked if we could take on his case as well. I explained to him that we could represent both of them only if they both waived the potential conflict of interest. This meant if we got to a point where either one were in the position of pointing a finger at the other, we would have to get out of both cases. He was sure his buddy would go along with this plan. He then left the office in the company of the game warden, to be taken back across the mountain to his home.

Some time later I was able to negotiate a plea agreement in

which the two men would each plead to a reduced charge calling for a one-year suspension of his hunting license, rather than the three-year suspension that would have followed from a conviction on the original charge. As we sat in my office, I explained the plea-bargain terms to them and they were agreeable. As the man who had first talked to me was about to leave, he said, "That game warden really doesn't like you, does he?" I joked that since I often represented people charged with fish-and-game violations, his question did not surprise me. "But," I said, "why do you ask?" He then told me the story of his return trip to Hancock after the session in my office.

As they were driving along, the game warden commented, "It's going to cost you a lot of money to hire Langrock and keep him in his expensive Italian suits." (It must be said I have never owned an Italian suit.) The game warden continued to talk, referring to me as a "gangster" and as a "person who had received stolen property." The stolen property he referred to grew out of "the great scallop-truck caper" described earlier. I had received a gift of five pounds of what turned out to be stolen scallops. After the young man's rendition of these conversations, I smiled and said that maybe we were being a bit premature to agree to a plea to the amended charge.

I made a phone call to Dick English, who was the state's attorney, and told him what happened. I told him I was planning to file a motion to dismiss the charges because of law-enforcement misconduct. It sounded like a good motion to me, although I knew of no basis for it in the rules other than in a general section where a judge has the right to enter a dismissal in the "interest of justice." I asked Dick if he would let me have a hearing on the motion without first informing the game warden involved what my client had told me. He agreed.

Some weeks later we had a hearing in the small room on the first floor of the courthouse, and Dick had the warden available for questioning. I called him to the stand and my first question was, "So, you think I'm a gangster, do you?" The game warden was visibly shaken. He admitted using that term, quickly adding, "Peter, I don't think you're really a gangster. I think you're a good lawyer. If I ever needed a lawyer, I'd hire you." We then went on to my "high-priced Italian suits" and the rest of the conversation he had had with my client.

Judge Frank Mahady, for whom our new courthouse is named, was on the bench. He and the court personnel present all enjoyed the game warden's testimony. In an order written the next day,

Mahady granted my motion to dismiss in this client's case, but refused to dismiss the case of his buddy. The judge agreed it was improper police practice to try to interfere with the relationship between a client and his attorney, especially at the level of the statements made by the warden. However, he held the second defendant had not been a party to the conversation, and the police misconduct did not carry over to him. This left me in the precarious position of having accomplished something for one client, but leaving his companion out to hang. Fortunately, Dick English agreed to a favorable resolution of the second case based upon a sense of fairness and the fact that no deer had actually been taken, the only violation being the carrying of the searchlight itself.

1. *State v. Bosworth,* 124 Vt. 3 (1963).
2. *State v. Quesnel,* 124 Vt. 491 (1965).
3. *Langrock v. Porter Hospital Inc.,* 126 Vt. 233 (1965).
4. *Woodard v. Porter Hospital, et al.,* 125 Vt. 264 (1965).
5. *Woodard v. Porter Hospital Inc., et al.,* 125 Vt. 419 (1966).
6. *State v. Stone,* 123 Vt. 95 (1962).
7. *Munson v. Goodro,* 124 Vt. 282 (1965).
8. *Zahn v. International Paper Company,* 53 F.R.P. 430 (Vt. 1971).
9. *Zahn v. International Paper Company,* 469 F.2d 1033 (1972).
10. *Zahn v. International Paper Company,* 469 F.2d 1033 (1972).
11. *Zahn v. International Paper Company,* 414 U.S. 291 (1973).
12. *Ouellette v. International Paper Company,* 602 F.Supp 264 (1985).
13. *Ouellette v. International Paper Company,* 776 F.2d 55 (1985).
14. *Ouellette v. International Paper Company,* 479 U.S. 481 (1987).
15. *State v. Kelly,* 131 Vt. 582 (1973).
16. *In Re: Rich,* 125 Vt. 373 (1966).
17. *State v. Rich,* 132 Vt. 523 (1974).
18. *State v. Demag,* 118 Vt. 273 (1954).
19. *Hackel v. Williams,* 122 Vt. 168 (1961).
20. *State v. Mahoney,* 122 Vt. 456 (1961).
21. *In Re: Estate of Howard Mahoney,* 126 Vt. 31 (1966).
22. *State v. Barrett,* 128 Vt. 458 (1970).
23. *State v. Barrett,* 130 Vt. 197 (1972).
24. *Pidgeon v. State Highway Board,* 147 Vt. 589 (1987).
25. *Langrock v. Department of Taxes,* 139 Vt. 108 (1980).
26. *State v. Zaccaro,* 154 Vt. 83 (1990).
27. *State v. Ballou,* 127 Vt. 1 (1968).

INDEX